Stumbli. . .

"This book is a rare gem: It combines a searing memoir with deep theological reflection, a unique genre that is all its own, which dates all the way back to Saint Augustine's *Confessions*. Josh has done the hard work of facing his troubled past and finding the thread of grace that has long made beauty from ashes. Many will resonate with the pain of his upbringing; even more will come alive at his vision of gospel hope."

> —JOHN MARK COMER, founding pastor of Bridgetown Church, teacher and writer with Practicing the Way, and bestselling author of *The Ruthless Elimination of Hurry* and *Live No Lies*

"*Stumbling Toward Eternity* is a bit like its author: intrepid and infectious, openhearted yet unflinching, and singularly focused on the grace of God for nontheoretical sinners. I can think of no better introduction (or pastoral handbook) to the endless mystery and radical generosity of the cross than what Josh has fashioned here—much of it out of his own ragged history. This book is redemption made plain, essential reading for anyone in need of real hope. And the footnotes alone are worth the price of admission! Now where's the soundtrack?!"

> —DAVID ZAHL, founder of Mockingbird Ministries and author of *Low Anthropology*

"Wow! What can't Josh White do? I've loved hearing him preach and sing, but now I've read his writing. And oh, what he writes about! The centrality of the cross, the pain of his father, the beauty of grace, the power of forgiveness, and the freedom available in Jesus. These pages hold deep theology, rich memoir, and a call to enter the life you were made for with God. Josh's vulnerability with his heartbreak and shortcomings will give you the courage to face your own head-on and discover there the presence of the crucified King."

—JOSHUA RYAN BUTLER, lead pastor of
Redemption Tempe and author of *Beautiful Union*
and *The Skeletons in God's Closet*

"*Stumbling Toward Eternity* is a genre-defining book. In this work of theology-as-memoir (or is it memoir-as-theology?), Josh White artfully interweaves his own story of trauma and healing with God's redemptive plan for all humanity. One cannot help but walk away from this text with a deeper sense of the never-ending grace and all-encompassing love of God, demonstrated not only in Jesus's words from the cross but also in how God uses human relationships to draw us close to Him. I hope this book will inspire many to do the hard work of integrating their own stories of sin and suffering into the much larger story of God's forgiveness and eternal love!"

—JAKE JOHNSON, PHD, LMFT, associate professor of
marriage and family therapy at Wheaton College

"Bestselling Christian books often hover just above the real stuff of our daily lives, hinting at but never fully touching the suffering, questions, and struggles most of us face. Josh White's *Stumbling Toward Eternity* can be described in various ways: compelling, faithful, engaging, hope-filled, beautifully written—but most of all, it is real. This book, like the grace it points us toward, embodies faith that keeps showing up in the gritty, earthy details of living and dying. Expect to cry and laugh and worship and to have a difficult time putting it down once you start reading it."

—MARK R. MCMINN, PHD, author of *The Science of Virtue: Why Positive Psychology Matters to the Church*

"*Stumbling Toward Eternity* is a story that weaves together the historical reality of Jesus's crucifixion and how Christ crucified brings healing, beauty, and redemption to our fragile humanity. Raw, honest, funny, and perhaps, most important, hopeful."

—RICK MCKINLEY, founding pastor of Imago Dei Community in Portland and author of *Faith for This Moment*

"My friend and fellow Portlander Josh White has given us a unique and poignant book, one that I couldn't put down once I began reading it. Combining deep exposition on the meaning of the cross of Christ with glimpses of Josh's painful past, *Stumbling Toward Eternity* defies easy description. My love and gratitude toward Jesus and my confidence in the power of the good news to save and transform was rekindled. Every page, including the footnotes, contained treasures, and I'll be returning to this book often."

—KEVIN PALAU, president of Luis Palau Association

"Josh White takes us into the very heart of Jesus's story, reminding us that His story is also ours. Part meditation, part memoir, and part theological reflection, this book will remind you that God is near the suffering and brokenhearted. God made us human but also took His own medicine. If there is no cross, there is no Christ. The suffering of Christ is our only hope."

—PATRICK SCHREINER, professor and author of
The Visual Word and Political Gospel

"Josh is who he says he is: 'serious about Jesus, obsessed with grace, and [holding] tenaciously to the centrality of the cross.' And more—he is a poet, songwriter and lyricist, down-to-earth theologian, and collector of wisdom. Yet it is his writing on suffering that captivated my whole soul. I read this book over and over, drinking in the reminders of the love of God, the stories of His people's suffering, and the confusion we all face when life goes bad. As I did, my chest filled again with that pain-defiant hope of all who encounter His comfort and strength in suffering. I dare say, this should be required reading for every follower of Jesus—and for every parent who hopes to raise passionate, resilient Jesus followers!"

—DIANE COMER, author of He Speaks in the
Silence and co-author of Raising Passionate
Jesus Followers

"For a decade I've known Josh White as a close friend, preacher, fellow musician, and now, author. Although Josh is a gifted leader with a naturally inquisitive mind, what I've loved most about Josh is his ongoing wholehearted fixation on Jesus and the power of His gospel. While this book gives a glimpse into Josh's heart, it also provides an expansive view of the ragged terrain of everyman's soul and the wounded healer who beckons us to His cross."

—JOSH GARRELS, independent musician and owner of Small Voice Records

"A mentor who Josh and I share describes 'compelling gospel witness' as that which tells the following two stories in tandem: *your* Jesus story and *the* Jesus story. Josh accomplishes this as beautifully as anyone I've heard. Many recent authors have written about the *why* and the *what* of Christianity (and the especially popular *how* under the banner of 'spiritual formation'). However, few have spoken so clearly and vulnerably to the *so what?* of Christianity. This is what *Stumbling Toward Eternity* does. This book will take its place next to the great classics penned by the cloud of witnesses who similarly and obsessively clung to Christ's cross through countless seasons of cultural upheaval and spiritual decline. My dear friend Josh is one of the most compelling witnesses to Jesus in my life. Read this book and you'll see why."

—EVAN WICKHAM, worship leader, songwriter, and lead pastor of Park Hill Church, San Diego

Stumbling Toward Eternity

Stumbling Toward Eternity

Losing & Finding Ourselves in the Cross of Jesus

Josh White

Foreword by Tim Mackie

MULTNOMAH

STUMBLING TOWARD ETERNITY

All Scripture quotations, unless otherwise indicated, are taken from the ESV® Bible
(The Holy Bible, English Standard Version®), copyright © 2001 by Crossway, a
publishing ministry of Good News Publishers. Used by permission. All rights reserved.
Scripture quotations marked (MSG) are taken from The Message, copyright © 1993, 2002,
2018 by Eugene H. Peterson. Used by permission of NavPress, represented by Tyndale
House Publishers. All rights reserved. Scripture quotations marked (NIV) are taken from
the Holy Bible, New International Version®, NIV®. Copyright © 1973, 1978, 1984,
2011 by Biblica Inc.™ Used by permission of Zondervan. All rights reserved worldwide.
(www.zondervan.com). The "NIV" and "New International Version" are trademarks
registered in the United States Patent and Trademark Office by Biblica Inc.™ Scripture
quotations marked (RSV) are taken from the Revised Standard Version of the Bible,
copyright © 1946, 1952, and 1971 National Council of the Churches of Christ in the
United States of America. Used by permission. All rights reserved worldwide.

Details in some anecdotes and stories have been changed to
protect the identities of the persons involved.

Copyright © 2023 by Josh White

All rights reserved.

Published in the United States by Multnomah, an imprint of
Random House, a division of Penguin Random House LLC.

MULTNOMAH® and its mountain colophon are registered trademarks of
Penguin Random House LLC.

Library of Congress Cataloging-in-Publication Data
Names: White, Josh, author.
Title: Stumbling toward eternity: losing and finding ourselves in the cross
of Jesus / Josh White.
Description: Colorado Springs, Colorado: Multnomah, [2023]
Identifiers: LCCN 2022031351 (print) | LCCN 2022031352 (ebook) |
ISBN 9780593193938 (trade paperback) | ISBN 9780593193945 (ebook)
Subjects: LCSH: Jesus Christ—Crucifixion. | Theology of the cross.
Classification: LCC BT450 .W48 2023 (print) | LCC BT450 (ebook) |
DDC 232.96/3—dc23/eng/20220902
LC record available at https://lccn.loc.gov/2022031351
LC ebook record available at https://lccn.loc.gov/2022031352

Printed in the United States of America on acid-free paper

waterbrookmultnomah.com

2 4 6 8 9 7 5 3 1

FIRST EDITION

SPECIAL SALES Most Multnomah books are available at special quantity discounts
when purchased in bulk by corporations, organizations, and special-interest groups.
Custom imprinting or excerpting can also be done to fit special needs. For information,
please email specialmarketscms@penguinrandomhouse.com.

*This book is dedicated to my muse,
best friend, and wife, Darcy;
to my beautiful children, Henry and Hattie;
and to the church I have pastored and
given the last thirteen years of my life,
Door of Hope in Portland, Oregon.*

We may very well take the cross as the symbol
at once of mystery and of health. . . .
The cross, though it has at its heart a collision
and a contradiction, can extend its four arms for
ever without altering its shape. Because it has a
paradox in its centre it can grow without changing. . . .
The cross opens its arms to the four winds;
it is a signpost for free travellers.

—G. K. Chesterton, *Orthodoxy*

FOREWORD

Sometimes you find a book that brings together topics, themes, and literary styles that are not usually combined and you think to yourself, *This is a special book.* This is that kind of book. Its uniqueness reflects the mind and heart of its author, Josh White, who is one of the most eclectic and creative humans I've ever encountered.

I first met Josh many years ago, when I joined him in pastoral ministry at Door of Hope, a church in Portland, Oregon, which he had started just a year and a half earlier. I soon discovered that Josh was not only a passionate pastor and teacher but also a talented musician and poet with a remarkable eye for interior design, and—on top of all that—he had read more in historical theology and classical western literature than anyone I'd ever met. But these are not the things that strike you most if you get to spend time with Josh. Rather, what you experience is his sincere enthusiasm and passion for following Jesus and for inviting other people to see how God's love can change everything in their lives.

This book is an excellent expression of all those things in one place. On its largest level, it's a thoughtful exposition of Jesus's last seven sayings He spoke from the cross. These words of Jesus have been close to Josh's heart for many years, and Josh has pondered their significance with great care and attentiveness. (In fact, the first sermon series Josh and I ever taught together, many years ago, was on these seven sayings of Jesus.) These writings are packed with thoughtful reflections on the teachings of Jesus and the power of the good news about Him. Along the way, you'll learn insights from theologians, poets, and philosophers that maybe you've heard of before but have probably never read.

But there's more going on in this book. Interwoven with these theological reflections are a series of memoir fragments that are deeply personal to Josh. Here you'll encounter a rare kind of raw vulnerability, as he shares about the pain and challenges he's faced in life, especially as it relates to his father. These stories are *crucial* to the purpose of the book. They reflect Josh's deep conviction that the love of Jesus can meet and transform us in our deepest experiences of pain, loss, and confusion. He truly believes that when we expose ourselves to God's love with total honesty and surrender, *that's* where we discover the healing power of the gospel.

I know that Josh would be thrilled if you learn a lot in the course of reading this book. But even more, his desire is that you have an encounter with the self-giving and suffering love of Jesus. He believes that love can address the most difficult and painful parts of our lives.

Thank you, Josh, for sharing your heart and mind with us in these pages. I hope that through this book many people are invited into a deeper experience with the life-transforming power of God's presence and love.

Tim Mackie

Co-founder of the BibleProject

CONTENTS

A WORD TO THE READER

The amateur—the lover, the man who thinks heedlessness
a sin and boredom a heresy—is just the man you need.
More than that, whether you think you need him or not,
he is a man who is bound, by his love, to speak. . . .

The role of the amateur: to look the world back to grace.

—Robert Farrar Capon, *The Supper of the Lamb*

Beginning is always an act of faith. The first step might be the most difficult. For me it is the fear of starting off on the wrong foot. I, like so many, suffer from what Jean Cocteau called "the agony of the act."*

So how does one begin a book? I suppose that I ought to begin with a word, which we could also call the theme: *love*. This four-letter word is as ubiquitous as it is misused and abused. But one cannot deny that however cliché, sentimental, or common it may be, it continues to be at the forefront of all human longing and meaning. So rather than abandon the word, I would like to qualify it with another: *grace,* which at its most basic level is *love without contingency.* Now I am getting ahead of myself, but the book has begun.

*Jean Cocteau, *The Difficulty of Being,* trans. Elizabeth Sprigge (New York: Melville House, 2013), 7.

Ever since reading *Tremendous Trifles* by G. K. Chesterton some twenty years ago, I have embraced the title of the amateur. In its most positive light, being an amateur simply means living in a state of childlike wonder. I am not suggesting a refusal to mature; there is a clear difference between being child*like* and being child*ish*. After all, Jesus did say, "Let the little children come to me . . . for to such belongs the kingdom of heaven."*

The word *amateur* comes from the Latin *amator,* which means "lover." My blessing and curse is that almost everything interests me. I tend to give myself to those interests with near obsession. I can love with a recklessness that can quickly overwhelm others, but whatever the downsides, this much is true: When I love, it is *sincere.*

Due to my love of libraries and disdain for classrooms, I might be appropriately called a lowbrow Renaissance man. I do my best to not take myself or the world too seriously, and I believe this is the best path for navigating the challenges of existence. Having said that, I am serious about Jesus, obsessed with grace, and hold tenaciously to the centrality of the cross.

Amateur also means I can be a scattered optimist. My mental glitches and complicated childhood make it extremely difficult to embrace a singular creative endeavor without feeling panicked and queasy. Being willing to dabble in nearly *everything* has led me to consider my

*Matthew 19:14.

life as simply an *unfinished event*. This leads to ideas often piling up and ultimately being forgotten. However, the ideas and interests that *do* make it out of my mind into "the real world" (as my wife calls it) are romanced with such passion that I become convinced everyone should be as enthusiastic as I am about the object of my affection. At least, until I am not. For much like Don Juan, once the romance is over, each passion is soon discarded for a new lover.

So let me just say, the quirkiness of my temperament has made bringing this book to completion more than a little challenging. I have faced an obsessiveness in choosing the right word, the right sentence, the right thought—driven by a desire to honor Jesus and represent Him and my orthodoxy well. I have agonized over the mining of my own broken history, my desire to merge grace and candor, without my mess somehow obstructing the view of His healing. All of this has led to the near destruction of my keyboard's delete key, as things have been written, erased, and rewritten, ad nauseam. The desire to jump ship has come more than I care to admit. While dealing with the stress of writing deadlines for which (like meetings) I am *never* on time, I've also been leading a church in Portland, Oregon, and the combination has counterintuitively led me to complete two unreleased albums and pick up tattooing and boxing as coping mechanisms. I've probably given my editor an ulcer (I do love you, Paul, and I am sorry) and my wife (Darcy, you are my gypsy queen) a headache.

The American poet Emily Dickinson once wrote her editor with a question as profound as it was anxious,

> Mr Higginson,
> Are you too deeply occupied to say if my Verse is
>   alive?
> The Mind is so near itself—it cannot see,
>   distinctly—and I have none to ask—
> Should you think it breathed—and had you
>   the leisure to tell me, I should feel quick
>   gratitude—*

In attempting to merge literary memoir and theological reflection, I have been haunted by that same question. I, like Emily, am too close to what is written to know if the words breathe and must rely on those around me who have spoken into this book. Since memoir and theology can react like oil and water, my way forward is fourfold.

First, I center on the *cross of Christ,* just as in life.

Second, I frame the book on the *seven words* Jesus spoke from the cross.

Third, I use memoir, or *fragments,* as I call them. This was the most difficult to incorporate. I selected memories that carried life-altering significance, as a way of understanding how the gospel interacts with our past,

---

*Dickinson to Thomas Wentworth Higginson, April 15, 1862, in Dickinson Electronic Archives, http://archive.emilydickinson.org/correspondence/higginson/l260.html.

present, and future. Memories are fragmentary by nature; they can be elusive, incomplete, menacing, and paradoxical, which makes turning them over carefully in the mind and writing what one sees as painful as it can be healing.

How they connect to the themes was not something that could be forced and often was more suggestive and nuanced as is life itself. My life is not a metaphor but at times can seem metaphorical. It's not a parable, though it may feel parabolic. It's not a cautionary tale, a tragedy, mystery, nightmare, romance, or adventure, but like every life, there are those archetypal and universal threads that tie us together in our shared humanity.

These fragments are not meant to explain the cross or interpret the words Jesus spoke from it. In fact, I believe it is the crucified King and His cross that interpret our stories, infusing them with the meaning we long for.

Fourth, I must also point out my use of *footnotes*. When they appear, the corresponding note will be on the bottom of the page itself. My mind loves to chase the interconnectedness of things, those threads that can open a door to meaning that was previously hidden or that may simply lead to a hallway that has no doors. They do not have to be read, but I hope you do, for often I found myself more excited about the footnote than the actual section that inspired it. (Such is the nature of the amateur.)

All that to say this: If you are reading these words, then the miraculous has happened—the book is done. I am likely breathing again. However, right now, in this moment, I am thinking about you, the reader. I am wondering who you might be and where you are in this crazy, unsettled world of ours. Even if this is as far as you read, let me just say to you what I say to our church every week because it's true: "On your worst day, Jesus is crazy about you!"

Grace upon grace over you and yours,

Josh

FIRST FRAGMENT

The Jump

[1982]

> He has made everything beautiful in its time. Also, he has put
> eternity into man's heart, yet so that he cannot find out what God
> has done from the beginning to the end.
>
> **—Ecclesiastes 3:11**

The apple tree next to the run-down apartment complex was huge. Some kids had salvaged a couple of dirty mattresses from the nearby dumpster and stacked them beneath the tree.

She was so cute—older than I was (probably eleven) and tall, with long dark hair. She wore an argyle sweater-vest over a plaid button-up shirt and high-waisted Jordache jeans. It was dusk. Her smile was glowing as she laughed at the boys jumping from the tree onto the mattresses. There I was in my Toughskin jeans, those stupid baby-poop brown suede shoes from Sears Roebuck, my "HOMEWORK BLOWS MY MIND" T-shirt, and an uneven, helmet-shaped haircut imposed on me by my mother (complete with a cowlick).

I watched the girl with unnoticed longing. Sam, my neighbor and only friend, was with me, so I decided to be brave. I climbed the tree to the very top. I looked down with hidden terror, made sure she was watching, and then before I could back out, I jumped.

The fall was fast, and the landing hard. Without even a bounce, my mouth connected with my knee, right where the hole in my jeans was, burying my front tooth into my kneecap. I held my leg and pulled my mouth free, groaning and wiping tears away as the blood began to flow.

But she noticed, she really *noticed,* and she even helped me up. I don't remember her name. I never saw her again. It didn't matter. For I had wrestled with God, and He had blessed me. I walked back to the apartment with a limp.

The Good Death & the Cross of Stumbling

But we preach Christ crucified, a stumbling block . . .

—1 Corinthians 1:23

For I decided to know nothing among you
except Jesus Christ and him crucified.

—1 Corinthians 2:2

The hardest thing in life is to live well. Perhaps that is why it is so hard to be honest about the difficulty of living.

The longer we live, the greater the enigma. The good news is there is nothing new under the sun. The mystery of life is still a shared mystery, and wherever the "human comedy" is told honestly, no matter how varied the experience, it carries universal truths. Our shared stories have the power to comfort us, remind us we are not alone, draw us out of ourselves, and point us to something bigger.

Take this book for example. Because of its personal nature and the insecurity it produces in me when I think about it being read, this book forces me to cling to the conviction that my ordinary life, like yours, *matters*. Our stories not only speak to the human experience but are woven into a singular story as well. Whether we are aware of it or not, this story permeates everything we know with divine significance. As G. K. Chesterton, a man who lived with what can be called a "sacramental cast"* (an ability to truly see the world through the lens of grace), wrote over a hundred years ago, "I had always felt life first as a story: and if there is a story, there is a story-teller."**

I believe in this larger story and in its Author's ability to weave the dissonant threads of our existence into His redemptive narrative, which has allowed me to begin to confront the dragon in the road—those wounds that have cut me so deeply that for much of my life, circumnavigation felt like the only viable option. Confronting them was simply too much.

It is my desire to not simply accept the truth but to allow the Spirit of truth to drive me to Jesus, who *is* the truth, again and again. To start is to stumble and maybe even fall. But no matter how painful the wounds we experience are (as well as the wounds we cause), they must be brought into the light and brought to the cross if we want to travel the path of Jesus.

*Harry Blamires, *The Christian Mind: How Should a Christian Think?* (London: S.P.C.K., 1963), 176.

**G. K. Chesterton, *Orthodoxy* (San Francisco: Ignatius, 1995), 66.

Why is it so hard to accept this? To believe that the gospel works not merely to remove our wounds but to transfigure them into something useful, even beautiful? Our wounds can be healed, and they can bring healing. It is true that they leave scars, but without those scars, what proof would we have of the healing?

God is calling His people back to the center, back to the *cross*. We are amid a cultural shaking that has left much of the church exposed and reeling. If we are to navigate these troubled times, we must relearn how to interpret the ideological battles raging around us through the lens of the gospel. If we remove the offense of the gospel, we lose Jesus. I am not at all suggesting we be offensive, but indifference should never be our goal. The Jesus who commanded His followers to "take up [your] cross and follow me" is being rapidly replaced with a new kind of Jesus who does not command but only suggests.*

If Jesus is stripped of His cross, His authority, and His power to forgive, heal, save, and judge, what are we left with? It's been said, "No cross, no crown," but in actuality it's "No cross, no *Christ*!"

It is my pressing conviction that if we diminish the cross of Christ, we drain Christianity of its lifeblood. Without the cross as the center, we will inevitably turn to what can be called ladder theology. Ladder theology is the default setting of human existence; it is the religious impulse in all of us to prove our worth through effort, to climb our

*Matthew 16:24.

way to a heaven that has already come down to us. The heroic ascent is a fool's errand. We can no more build to the heavens than we can save ourselves, and all our attempts to do so will end in self-deception and ruin. As followers of Jesus, we cannot afford to forget what the early church fathers called the "kenosis," or self-emptying, of King Jesus. As Paul said in the letter to the Philippians,

> Have this mind among yourselves, which is yours in Christ Jesus, who, though he was in the form of God, did not count equality with God a thing to be grasped, but emptied himself, by taking the form of a servant, being born in the likeness of men. And being found in human form, he humbled himself by becoming obedient to the point of death, even death on a cross. Therefore God has highly exalted him and bestowed on him the name that is above every name.*

Our satisfaction will never be found on the ladder of human effort. Instead, it will be found in our daily surrender to the One who descended into the depths of human brokenness, emptied Himself of His glory, and identified with us at our lowest point, our sin, all without collapsing under its weight. The glory of God can no longer be defined by His impenetrable otherness or the insurmountable distance between Himself and the creation

*Philippians 2:5–9.

He sustains. His glory is discovered most fully at the foot of the cross, in His humiliation. For this is where the crucified God eradicated once and for all the impossible distance between Himself and His rebellious human creation. Our acceptance of a work that cannot be improved upon is the only way we will ascend.

The path is always down before Jesus can lift us up.

. . .

Anyone familiar with the history of crucifixion as a method of execution must acknowledge that on the surface, the cross—an instrument of horrific torture and capital punishment—is a strange choice for the central emblem of the Christian faith. Widely used by the Romans as a public deterrent for revolt and crime, crucifixion was considered the cruelest and most grotesque of punishments. It was reserved solely for the lowest criminals and slaves. Paradoxically, the Romans, who prided themselves on their civility and order, refused to take ownership for the barbaric and obscene invention of crucifixion; they found its cruelty distasteful to even discuss in polite company.

It is difficult for us to understand the scandal of the cross today. As a symbol, it has become so sanitized of its original purpose that it is almost impossible for us to understand its cruelty. It was a device created by the wrath of man, meant to obliterate with brutal simplicity all semblance of its victim's humanity. The sight, sound, and

smell of this prolonged public torture—where the crucified hung naked, sometimes for days, soiled, and bloody,
incapable even of stopping hungry birds from feeding on
their totally exposed flesh—were meant to overwhelm the
senses and strike fear in both the crowd and the crucified.

It makes sense that Paul referred to the cross as a
"stumbling block."* There is something offensive about
a seemingly helpless, humiliated man dying the death of a
common criminal and then being called the King of kings,
the Savior of the world, a perfect man, and our holy God.
Yet for Christians, the cross and its crucified God-man lie
at the center of all meaningful discourse.

Why? How? Because the heartbeat of the gospel is not
the wrath of God but the *love* of God. His wrath is simply
His love violated. This is the God who "so loved the
world, that he gave his only Son."** In the cross, God
takes the worst that humanity can produce—an instrument of total hatred and cruelty—and commandeers it.
Love transforms this instrument of torment into a vehicle
for God's best, His saving grace.

There is much in the crucifixion of Jesus that is wrapped
in mystery, what Scripture calls the hidden things of
God.*** However, there is also much that has been revealed. Though the exact mechanics of atonement continue to be a source of much theological debate, what

*1 Corinthians 1:23.

**John 3:16.

***See Matthew 11:25.

can be known dimly has the power to illuminate our lives in such a way that all things become new. For the very One who died for us also explained what He was doing while He was dying.

There were seven "words," as they are traditionally called, recorded in the four Gospels, which were spoken by Jesus as He hung from the cross of Calvary. In each statement, Jesus—who is the *logos,* the Living Word, which is "sharper than any two-edged sword"*—brings a death blow to the lies that keep us from Him. Yet it is through these same words we find resurrection life. It is at the cross we discover we are inexorably loved, and it is at the cross we discover the freedom to love.

I have come up horribly short, yet God has chosen in His freedom to love me, die for me, forgive me, and save me, using the brokenness in my life to re-create me. Thus He reveals the holy mystery of His unwillingness to exist without broken people like me. How can I not thank Him for this gift? True, I do not thank Him for the abandonment, abuse, or anxiety I have experienced throughout my life. I'm not a masochist and neither is God. I see them for what they are—the outcome of sin within and without—but I do thank Him (though not nearly enough) for His ability to work through these difficulties to bring beauty out of the ashes.

Now it may seem primitive, one might even say offensive, to speak so passionately about the murder of a Jew-

*Hebrews 4:12.

ish teacher who lived two thousand years ago. A man who claimed to be one with God with such consistency that anyone seriously looking into the claims of Jesus is forced into a corner where a decision is required. Either He was God then, which means He is God now, or He was a madman who, by some strange twist of fate and sleight of hand, accidentally set world history on fire. If the latter is true, He is—metaphorically speaking, of course—laughing in His grave at the lengths we will go to diminish our anxieties that life in all of its exhausting complexity and stifling brevity produces. But how can anyone gaze into the face of Jesus for any length of time and not be fixated by the miraculous merger of such gentleness and fierceness, humility and power, suffering and peace, justice and love? All I can say is, if Jesus is not the Son of God, then I must worship the ones who invented Him.

For when I come to the cross, I am silenced, the curse is revealed and reversed, and my illusions are exposed and overthrown. This is the place where our stories are brought into the light. Yes, this is the place where original sin is replaced by what is more original still: *Grace*.

This cross is the center from which we stumble toward eternity.

1.

The Cross of Judgment & Forgiveness

_____

The First Word from the Cross

_____

When they came to the place that is called The Skull,
there they crucified him, and the criminals, one on his
right and one on his left. And Jesus said, "Father,
forgive them, for they know not what they do."

—Luke 23:33–34

The Wounded Hand & the Clenched Fist

Forgiveness saves. Forgiveness reconciles.
Forgiveness must permeate our politics again; forgiveness
and not moral codes; forgiveness and not Moses-zeal!
For forgiveness alone makes it possible for us to live
together. Forgiveness alone heals wounds.
Forgiveness does not make void the laws of God;
no indeed, it teaches us to keep them.

—Karl Barth, *Come, Holy Spirit: Sermons*

No words have haunted me with such paradoxical beauty like the first recorded words that fell from the lips of Jesus as He hung in agony, naked and beaten beyond recognition. Not even the crowd's derision could silence the two-edged sword that He spoke from His parched and bloody lips. This was His heart of mercy spoken over and against the blinding violence of alienated humanity.

It is here we find the God of *yes* with His reconciliation on display through Jesus the suffering servant. This is forgiveness not requested but personified and proclaimed. Jesus's open and pierced hands are contrasted against the clenched fists of the hateful mob,* absorbing the vitriol and violence of human history. Jesus's glory is revealed in His humiliation. The *elective love* of God is on display. He chooses—for He alone is truly free—to love sinners in their sin. He is a forgiving God because He is love. Neither forgiveness nor wrath is a part of His essential nature; rather they are the outcome of His holy character violated. We have done much, known and unknown, that needs forgiveness. Ignorance is not innocence, but the good news that falls from the forsaken God's lips is that He is a God of mercy. In the anguish, there was also the joy set before Him, which is you. This is judgment and re-creation. This is the great exchange: Our sin blotted out through His spilled blood. This is the Judge who was judged in our place. It is the heart of the

---

*The clenched fist has always been a symbol of revolution, resistance, and often violence. Amid revolution, socialist parties used it commonly in the twentieth century. It was adopted by the black power, or nationalist, movement of the sixties (most notably the Black Panthers), and it reemerged with the Black Lives Matter movement of today. It is also used by white nationalist groups. I am not here to speak into the ideologies of these various movements, but I will address the shared meaning of the fist they use symbolically. Solidarity and unity are the most common words connected to the symbol of the fist today. But that is misleading at best, for we must ask, "Solidarity to what?" and "By what means?" The clenched fist was at the center of the most violent century in human history and has been primarily used as a unifying rally to revolution by those who saw themselves as oppressed. Oppressed or not, there is rage behind this symbol. In fact, in the history of the revolutions that used this emblem, most often the result was not peace but even more violent regimes. Why? Because violence begets violence. The closed fist is used to punch, not embrace, and it is an emblem of anger, not forgiveness. It is hard not to contrast it with the passive resistance movements of MLK or Gandhi, who never raised fists but fought by surrender. But nothing compares to the revolution of love worked by the pierced, open hands of King Jesus.

Father being revealed through the Spirit-filled Son's aton-
ing work. He does not need us, but He is not content to
exist without us. To be forgiven is to be embraced by the
forgiving God. To be forgiven is to be freed to forgive and
love.

You Didn't Want to Be with Me

[1975]

A dysfunctional family is any family
with more than one person in it.

—Mary Karr, *The Liars' Club*

He watched with unblinking eyes, too large for
his disheveled head. He was clinging so tightly
to his teddy that his hands had turned a whitish blue.
He was staring, alone in his fear, out of a dirty window from the back seat of his father's run-down car
at a volatile scene he did not understand. You could
hear his heartbeat almost as loudly as his parents'
muffled screams while he watched the scene
through tears. His mother was hitting his outraged
father like a wild animal.

This is my earliest memory. It's vivid but silent
when I play through it in my mind, like an out-of-
body experience, which makes it all the more unsettling.

When I was one, my parents had divorced. On

this visit, Dad was drunk and had put me in the back of his car. Mom later told me I kept crying, "Please don't let him take me, Mommy!" while my father yelled, "He is my son too!" I can see the scene, but I do not hear it. What is etched upon my mind is two people fighting over me, in front of me, while I am invisible. Despite the silence of this remembered event, even today I find the emotions of it are still present and impactful.

. . .

Forty-four years later, while I was visiting my father in his run-down, filthy, cigarette-stained home in rural Alaska, he brought up that incident. Between drags of Camel Red and sips of vodka, with greasy hair stuck to his forehead and a highly flammable breathing tube in his nose, Dad spoke to me. The words came in his crackling baritone voice that never seems to have enough air: "I am still pissed at you for that, Joshua!"

"Pissed at me for what?"

"That you didn't want to be with me!"

"I was two!"

"I am still pissed!"

As with most conversations with my father these days, this dialogue came suddenly to an end. There was a stilted and abrupt quality to his speech, as it moved without warning between nostalgia, worry, agitation, and sudden silence. I am sure this was due to a lifetime of substance abuse and years of isolation. Words were spoken and then abandoned as he retreated into an interior solitude that matched the loneliness of the Alaskan landscape around him.

How could he say that to me? The words pressed down on me with a near-otherworldly significance—not because they were true but because they were honest. He felt rejected, angry, and alone; he had pushed those feelings down and hid. Now, finally, he had confessed. He had released his grievance, and we were left with the sadness and absurdity of the words. His statement stood between us—as cold and oppressive as the permanent twilight and sub-zero weather outside. But as I sat in the discomfort of that smoke-filled space, an understanding began to slowly wash over my frustration in what I can only describe as a holy intervention. As Dad stared out the window at the snow-covered ground, fighting to breathe, I saw him in his brokenness as a child, and there I found compassion. My lips unlocked and my tongue loosened: "I am sorry, Dad."

"It's okay, Joshua. I'm just having a hard time at the moment, son."

"I know, Dad. I love you."

"I love you too, son. I'm glad you're here. Your old man is usually tougher than this."

"I know, Dad."

End of conversation.

And there was peace mingled in the sadness as we sat there, quietly watching one of Dad's favorite shows, *Little House on the Prairie*. There on the screen was Pa Ingalls, pleading in a field for God to save his son. It seemed like some strange portent, and I silently pleaded the same for my dad.

Forgiveness, Where Are You?

Grace means that God does some quite definite thing,
not a thing here and a thing there, but something quite definite
in men. Grace means that God forgives men their sins.

—Karl Barth, *The Epistle to the Romans*

Forgiveness is a word dimly understood, challenging to define, and even more difficult to give or receive. It is a ghost of days gone by that holds very little bearing in the age of victimization with all its demands for justice. It's not that it is thought about with disdain; it's just not really thought about at all. To use our modern mode of quantification, it is not a word that is currently trending.

If it does make its way into our collective consciousness, it is used primarily to describe what is out of reach. In pop music, it often describes a longing to correct what is already over—in other words, "too little too late." If the word is uttered in film or on television, it comes in the form of a frantic request that seems to guarantee its denial. The hero or antihero is about to unleash vengeance

on some sad sack who is about to expire and is patheti-
cally crying out, "I'm sorry, forgive me." There are those
passing scenes of the shady priest in the confessional box
offering absolution from a God who is portrayed as not
present.*

Outside of communities of faith, the most common
and innocuous use of the word *forgiveness* is found in the
home (at least in my limited experience). My wife, Darcy,
and I continually spoke about forgiveness as we braved
those exhausting but beautiful early years of parenting. In
that formative season for our two magical children, Henry
and Hattie, we found ourselves frequently offering forgiveness to them or requesting it from them. They most
likely never asked for this absolution, and they didn't understand what it was they were granting. I am personally
so prone to mishap that being quick to ask for forgiveness
has been my only defense.** I can't tell you how many
times, as a means of consoling after a correction or comforting after unmanaged irritation, I spoke these words:

*The film industry's seeming commitment to a two-dimensional presentation of
Christianity as a monolithic movement marked by sociopaths, prigs, prudes, and
perverts is as maddening as it is false. But before we point the finger at Hollywood
for its cheap shots, let's at least acknowledge the nauseating sentimentality, lack of
artistry, and oversimplification of complex issues found in so much of what we
would call Christian entertainment.

**I had the gift of chaos when the kids were little, and most of the time it was silly
and fun, until it wasn't, such as the time I asked Henry if he wanted to see something
funny while we waited in the car for Darcy and Hattie. I honked the horn as they
were walking in front of it, scaring them to death (they are both highly sensitive
persons). My wife was so enraged that her middle finger went flying. In her gritted
teeth and glare, I could see my own execution take place, while my four-year-old
collapsed into an inconsolable puddle of tears. Sorry, ladies, I feel bad that it still
makes me smile.

"It's okay, Hanky. Daddy forgives you, but you can't take Sister's toy from her when she is playing with it."

"Miss Hattie, I love you and I forgive you. So does Henry, but you cannot hit him when you're frustrated. Okay? Now tell Brother you're sorry."

"Oh, Hattie, I am so sorry. Daddy didn't mean to scare you like that. Will you forgive me, baby?"

"Buddy, I am so sorry. I got frustrated, and that's not okay. I love you so much! Will you forgive me?"

I can't think of a single time when young Henry or Hattie ever said, "Daddy, forgive me." At most, I received the slowly spoken, "Sorry," which was usually prompted by, "What do we say?"* The point is this: My kids never felt the need to ask for something they instinctively knew I would give them. My requests for forgiveness from them have never been because their love for me was at stake. I ask for their forgiveness for the same reason I ask God for a forgiveness that is already mine: To humble my naturally proud, excuse-making self.

We can teach our children what is right and wrong, we can help them understand sin and lovingly discipline them, but if grace rules the home, forgiveness becomes the air they breathe. Forgiveness, like air, cannot be explained to a child, only experienced. We, the parents,

---

*I can only speak from my own parenting experience. Due to the mess of my childhood—though my mom loved us fiercely—I am well aware that what I am saying is not the experience of every child. It is heartbreaking and unbearable to think of children being neglected and abused. If you are like me, our healing is found at the cross. There the acceptance of forgiveness and the willingness to truly forgive forge the ability to tell a different story.

absorb the unfiltered emotions and unpredictable behavior: The food on the floor, the diaper artwork, the bald spot on the dog, the permanent marker on the face, the tantrums, the fork in the outlet, the hitting, biting, and scratching. They literally can be little beasts. I know there were times my wife and I—especially Darcy, who carried the bulk of this load—were exhausted, overwhelmed, and even longed for a momentary respite provided by Mimi and Papa, but nothing could separate Henry and Hattie from our love, then or now. Forgiveness was the fact, not the focus of conversation in our home. For us, the "yes" of love was simultaneously the corrective "no" to the wrongs that could never threaten it, as well as the covering that left guilt, shame, and fear suffocated and forgotten.

I am not attempting to say we don't need to ask for forgiveness from God. We should. I am saying that unless we become like little children, our requests will remain unreal. Why? Because it is childlike faith—the belief that we are loved without condition—that causes us to confess. As I said at the beginning, this is a book about love. Love defined by grace, and grace is love without contingencies. The forgiveness of Jesus is not mere pardon; it is His acceptance of us as His beloved, in spite of us. It can be as difficult to receive as it is to define, but there is not a person who has truly experienced it that didn't know it when it came. Why? Because we don't just experience forgiveness, we experience the God who forgives.

The Judge &
the Judged

Just as we can never go behind God's saving and revealing acts in
Jesus Christ and in the mission of his Spirit, so we can never think
or speak of him truly apart from his revealing and saving acts or
behind the back of Jesus Christ, for there is no other God.

—Thomas F. Torrance, *The Christian Doctrine of God*

Understanding the words "Father, forgive them"* requires
that we ask, What kind of statement is this? Is it a plea, a
request, or a proclamation? And, what has God revealed
Himself to be like? First and foremost, God is revealed in
Scripture as one. But as the revelation of Scripture un-
folds, the one God reveals Himself to be a community
within Himself, as Father, Son, and Holy Spirit. We worship and serve a triune God. The moment we forget that,
our entire faith can unravel like a snag in a sweater. We
may not be able to explain the Trinity, but God's triune
nature is what makes sense of everything else.**

*Luke 23:34.

**Let's consider something else that can't be understood but is itself the foundation
to understanding other things that would be hidden: Quantum mechanics. A subfield

We must not separate the mind of the eternal Son from that of the Father and the Spirit. It is tempting to apply to Jesus the relationship we see between God and Moses, who asked the Lord to show the rebellious Israel-ites mercy. In that account, we are told that "the LORD relented."* God moved from severity to mercy based upon Moses's mediation. Jesus is indeed our mediator. He is the final mediation, and God does get angry. He hates sin because it violates His character and robs Him of what He loves: You! The problem with comparing this to the cross is that it divides the triune God into compet-ing persons. The gentle Son is not pleading with an angry Father. He is presenting the heart of a Father who loves us despite ourselves. This is fundamentally the most trans-formative truth for me. My Christian life did not begin to open up until I truly believed in the depth of my being that on my worst day, Jesus is crazy about me. It's not just Jesus but the triune God who loves and who is love. As Jesus said to His disciples in the upper room, "Whoever has seen me has seen the Father."**

---

of physics that describes the behavior of atoms, quantum mechanics continues to this day to baffle scientists with its hazy probabilities and violations of time and space. It flies in the face of reality itself. Yet we know it to be real because it is the entire basis for the computer and semiconductor, to name just a couple of examples. So too, the doctrine of the Trinity brings harmony and clarity to God's self-disclosure, His redemptive history, and what it means to be made in the image of God. At the same time, the fact that God is three in one in inseparable unity is a mystery hidden within God Himself. Attempts to dispose of this impenetrable doctrine—and many have tried—unravel the heart of the Christian faith and create endless heretical prob-lems and contradictions, which the Trinity in all its apparent contradictions actually solves.

*Exodus 32:14.

**John 14:9.

We cannot pit persons of the triune God against each other without doing damage to the Godhead itself. Jesus is the man who mediates and the God who forgives, the judge and the judged in our place. He is communicating the Father's heart because He and the Father are one. As it is declared in the letter of Hebrews,

> In the past God spoke to our ancestors through the prophets at many times and in various ways, but in these last days he has spoken to us by his Son, whom he appointed heir of all things, and through whom also he made the universe. The Son is the radiance of God's glory and the exact representation of his being.*

God has nothing to say to us except what He has said and continues to say through Christ, who is the Word become flesh. Jesus is the final Word and the eternal solution to God's pursuit of humanity in our brokenness and sin. He is consistent with what we see from Genesis to Revelation: God is a God who continually intervenes in humanity's brokenness. The forgiveness that is proclaimed in the Scriptures corresponds to the work of the cross. The good news is that God, in His freedom, chooses to love sinners in their sin. This is grace. This is God with us and for us. Jesus is not wrestling with the Father's reluctance but proclaiming His heart to forgive. There is no God behind the back of Jesus.

*Hebrews 1:1–3, NIV.

Scripture is graphic in its depiction of God's forgiveness. His forgiveness is more than simply pardon. It is removal: "As far as the east is from the west, so far has he removed our transgressions from us."*

This is not a self-induced amnesia. Rather, God has chosen to put our sin aside as if it never happened. The vivid language of that scripture emphasizes the completeness of God's forgiveness. When He forgives, our sins are dealt with thoroughly. God sees them no more. He sees us in His Son, the sinless one. The forgiving God, in His freedom, has chosen to love us and cleanse us through His love. He is holy love. His goal is not pardon but acceptance of the sinner, and our God is a consuming fire.

*Psalm 103:12, NIV.

The Mole

[1979]

For all have sinned and fall short of the glory of God.

—Romans 3:23

It was a hot summer day. The air was stagnant as the old man, who sold night crawlers for a living, sat in his lawn chair with a shotgun across his lap, waiting for the mole to surface. We were picking blackberries beneath the shadow of the bridge when we heard the shot from behind us. We licked our purple-stained fingers, dropped our buckets, and ran toward that lonely, windblown man. He stood triumphantly over the mound that he had been angrily watching from his manicured lawn. To his surprise, and maybe embarrassment, the poor, blind subterranean dweller had surfaced, from the confusion and vibration of the blast, unscathed. Miraculously, the spread of pellets had missed it.

The old man called us kids closer and let us hold

and pet the docile alien creature. It had brown vel-
vetlike fur, a seemingly eyeless face, a pink nose,
and strange two-thumbed, oversized paws that
turned outward, allowing it to move through the dirt
like a swimmer performing the breaststroke.

The shift from the dark earth to the open air utterly
transformed its behavior. For in our hands, its soft-
ness both in touch and temperament made it impossible for us to grasp that beneath the ground it was a
monster, a destroyer of earth that terrorized the
man's precious earthworms with its poisonous saliva
and awful clown paws, which could grasp its victim
with such precision so as to squeeze the dirt out of
its insides without killing it, carrying the prey back to
its larder for later consumption.

The old man could not allow this, because the
earthworms were his livelihood and the yard their
home, which is why when we were done playing
with our temporary pet, he took it behind his house
and shot it in the head.

. . .

It's not just the violence of the story that haunts me.
It's not even the paradoxical nature of the mole—
although both are poignant. It is how the whole narrative is haunted by the groan of creation itself. Even
as a child I sensed that creation was a gift that had
somehow gone wrong. That day held beauty, joy,

play, and wonder, yet there was something else—
something ominous that cast a shadow over us as
fully as the cantilever bridge shadowed the yard.
The allure of death is one of the unsettling pieces. As
children, we had heard the gun before, so we knew
what it did. We had never seen anything move after
it had been on the receiving end of that old man's
shotgun. We were thrilled to see the mole alive, but
we were also ready to witness, and even participate
in, its death. Then there is the old man, frail and
close to death, but willing to waste his days, with-
drawn, violently protecting what he felt was his livelihood, when in actuality it did not provide enough
to take care of his most basic needs but nonetheless
was his identity. He didn't have time for life; he was
too busy protecting it from unseen threats. There is
also the duality of the mole itself. In the ground it
was hidden in darkness, violent and elusive, but the
light of its new environment instantly transformed its
very nature. Yet, if given a choice, it would return to
the dark.

I, like you, am a part of this grand narrative. In
the light of the crucified King, I have come to recognize the invisible thread that weaves it together. I
am innocence lost, and yet I am still full of childlike
wonder. I am the aging man who wastes life to
avoid death's coming, and yet I am also wisdom
growing. I am the mole, both monster and new
creation, hidden and exposed, dangerous and

gentle. My existence is always a potential gift or threat to others. I am both of the earth and the air. I am heaven and hell. I am a mixture. But unlike the mole that died once, I must die that good death daily.

The Sinfulness of Sin & the Law of Mixture

GOD sticks his head out of heaven. He looks around.
He's looking for someone not stupid—one man,
even, God-expectant, just one God-ready woman.
He comes up empty. A string of zeros.

—Psalm 14:2–3, MSG

Our denial of sin has done nothing to curb its cosmic fecundity. It has merely created an inability to explain why we hurt and where we can find healing. It has led to the current culture of victimization. Understanding sin and mixture in our own lives is what will set us free from being the victim or blaming the victimizer. Everyone will be both in their lives, and Jesus died for both. Jesus, in the Sermon on the Mount, does not just disturb our victim narrative today but utterly dismantles it with three words when He says to His disciples, "If you then, *who are evil*, know how to give good gifts to your children, how much more will your Father who is in heaven give good things to those who ask him!"*

*Matthew 7:11, emphasis added.

As Jesus was speaking to His followers about prayer, He made this rather offensive statement without explanation. His reference to them as evil, but capable of good, is as troubling as it is profound. It is a word that sheds light on the purpose of His entire message and why He came. It is also the crux to understanding this book. The coexistence of evil alongside good is a baffling idea for us since we tend to define *evil* as something we are not. It is a word we reserve for the worst that humanity produces. We are so gifted at deflection. Jesus, however, does not separate humanity into various groups based on effort. Nor does He suggest His disciples are as bad as they could be. No, for Jesus there seem to be only two groups:

1. Evil people who say yes to His yes, accepting His sacrifice on their behalf.

2. Evil people who say no to His yes, rejecting His sacrifice on their behalf, which I would argue is the blasphemy of the Holy Spirit.

It is easy to see how damaging the Sermon on the Mount could be if we do not understand its purpose. We can no more live what He demands than He can sin. We are damned without the cross, for we can't be perfect. It's the whole reason He came. His words are meant to bring us to the end of ourselves. Like the alcoholics or drug addicts who have bottomed out and recognize they can't do it without help, the Christian life flows from the same principle. It is our daily surrender to the sinless Christ by His Spirit within us that brings the change. Yet we hammer people with the sermon's impossible demands, attempting to externalize it when the root problem is that of the heart.

As one example, and I could give many, one may practice nonviolence, but Jesus said anger at another person is murder. For me, there isn't a day that goes by where I don't kill someone—even people I love.* You might be asking, "What about righteous indignation?" Yes, but our mixture means that righteousness in our anger cannot be sustained. We cannot hold our anger the way that God does, which is why Scripture warns us: "Do not let the sun go down while you are still angry, and do not give the devil a foothold."**

There is a fundamental brokenness that lies beneath the surface of everything. Unfortunately, when we refuse to recognize the implications of sin—not only in the world but also in our lives as believers—the outcome is an inevitable movement away from the cross and back to the ladder. Ladder and law are interchangeable. Ladder theology is the false belief that if I achieve A, B, and C, then I will be accepted and satisfied and then I will prove my worth. All people engage in it, but it is most disturbing in the church. Why? Because it manifests in our attempts

---

*Portland, as of late, has unfortunately turned my imagination into something more akin to the scenes of ultraviolence from *Clockwork Orange* than the still waters and green pastures of Scripture.

**Ephesians 4:26–27, NIV.

to present to the world an ideal that we ourselves can't live. We would never say this, but it's what we communicate when we view behavior and traditions as the defining factors of our faith. The ladder is defined by the false promise of arriving by climbing. The cross is defined by the promise of knowing by dying.

Ladder theology leads to what I like to call selective sanctification. And it's not just a Christian problem. It is a universal phenomenon—I was guilty of it before I was saved and still find myself wanting to do it today. Selective sanctification reduces life to a list of personal convictions to create a sense that we are okay in the world. It is driven by our dueling desires to belong and to hide. The heartbreaking reality is that when this goes unchecked among believers it leads to lovelessness and pride in the pulpit, judgment and exhaustion in the pew, scandal and damage in the church, and ineffectiveness in the world.

This is why we must not downplay the seriousness of our sin nature (*singular*) from which the endless variations of our sins (*plural*) play out. The Lord's words remind us that we are often ignorant of the darkness within. I can wake up a zealot, by the afternoon be a hedonist, and end my day like a practical atheist. We need the Spirit's illumination to look at the sin in ourselves and the mixture it creates. For at its most elemental level, sin is . . .

1. A *universal rebellion* against God's rule and a continual rejection of His grace: "I am my own!" "My will be done!"

2. *Sickness and slavery.* What is clear in Scripture (and
   is played out in crushing real time throughout
   human history) is that sin is invasive, and it infil-
   trates every arena of human existence. Sin has dis-
   torted what it means to be made in the image of
   God. The image is still present, but it has been
   deeply marred, leaving humanity bound, broken,
   blind, and in need of divine intervention. It doesn't
   mean that everything we do is bad, but it does
   mean—even for those who have been regenerated—
   that everything we do is mixture. There is much
   that needs to be forgiven, and ignorance is not innocence. At its core, sin is us playing God, and
   nothing enslaves like the tyranny of the illusory or,
   as I prefer to call it, the shadow self.

As Jesus Himself said, "Very truly I tell you, everyone
who sins is a slave to sin. Now a slave has no permanent
place in the family, but a son belongs to it forever. So if
the Son sets you free, you will be free indeed."*

But what does that freedom look like if sin is always a
problem? To answer that we must consider the law of
mixture.

. . .

The law of mixture is a truth that is as ubiquitous as it is
ignored and denied. The difficulty of *being* lies in the in-

*John 8:34–36, NIV.

escapable fact that no matter where we live, how young or old we are, who we love or who we've lost, what we have or don't have, how wise or unaware we are, and even what we believe or don't believe, until we *shuffle off this mortal coil,* life at its best is mixture.

It's amazing how the world ignores this truth. But it is especially confounding when Christians do so since it describes the inescapability of our sin nature and its impact on every arena of existence. *Mixture.* It is everywhere. It is in us. This is a hard and sobering truth, capable of creating bitterness, anger, and despair if it is not anchored in the gospel of Jesus. When the Spirit first confronted me with this truth, I was brought to my knees and met with grace. It has been my key to understanding the impossibility of life without losing hope, and it has helped me, though far from perfectly, to enter into my suffering and the suffering of others, such as my father. Most importantly, it has been a continual reminder that the goal of the Christian life is not arriving but *knowing*.

Of course, I am not the first to describe this law. I think of the apostle Paul, who wrote, "So I find this law at work: Although I want to do good, evil is right there with me."*

Wherever I am, I find mixture with me. It is within me, beside me, behind me, and before me. Its inflexible nature is written into the fabric of creation—this is why all of creation groans—and it cannot be escaped without escaping life itself. Wrestling with this truth is not for the

*Romans 7:21, NIV.

faint of heart, and there is as much danger in overanalysis as there is in avoidance of this reality.

Our frustration and madness flow out of life's apparent incompleteness. One could say we are frustrated with the frustration held within the gift of existence itself. The dark side of mixture (death, failure, loss, suffering), like an unwanted companion, is always there to remind us just how fragmented we are. This universal longing to be both more and the same is insatiable. This is the paradox of existence—we want to be "ourselves" but never seem to be satisfied with the self we currently are. Our mixture does not dissipate as Christians; in fact, it is amplified by Christ's very presence. This is why the apostle Paul, at the end of his life, wrote to the young pastor Timothy, "Christ Jesus came into the world to save sinners, of whom I am the foremost."* Notice, he said "I am" a sinner, not "I was." Why? Because intimacy with Jesus means living in the light, and we can't come into the light without being continually exposed. One of the great and painful lessons I am still learning is that the victory I have in Christ is not the conquering of my mixture. It is the victorious Christ, working in and through my mixture because, in His loving freedom, He chooses to do so. The question I must ask daily is, Am I willing to actually surrender this glitchy vehicle called me to its rightful owner?

Sin is forgiven but that doesn't mean forgiven sins aren't treacherous due to our mixture. There is a perpetual con-

*1 Timothy 1:15.

flict of the new nature—*Christ in me*—at play within a sinful setting. For no matter how much I sense the Spirit of Christ at work, or no matter how effectively and boldly the gospel is proclaimed, there is simultaneously a plethora of other voices in the back of my head—calling me a fraud, singing my praise, pointing out my shortcomings, and inflating my strengths. This is why the cross must remain our center, for without it we will always try to downplay or ignore the mixture that is always at play. As theologian Gerhard Forde warned, "Superficial optimism breeds ultimate despair."*

But if we are forgiven, why do we still struggle? Maybe it's because we treat forgiveness as an end in itself rather than the outcome of the end, the once-and-for-all work of the cross. The Spirit must grieve over our distrust in the forgiveness that is already ours. His atonement is a finished event that has secured the forgiveness of humanity, but we must say yes to His yes over us if we want to experience this reality. His forgiveness cannot be separated from Himself. The challenge before us is the fact that the default setting of the human heart is to push back against anything that threatens our autonomy. Forgiveness of sins is not the purpose of the cross, for God has always been a forgiving God. The purpose of the cross is reconciliation, by which the gulf between God and man has been permanently removed through Christ's victory over sin,

*Gerhard O. Forde, *On Being a Theologian of the Cross* (Grand Rapids, Mich.: Eerdmans, 1997), 16.

death, and the dominion of darkness. The gift is not simply forgiveness; it is the forgiving God Himself who chooses to love us in our sin but is not content to leave us there. Absolution is total on the side of God, and it is rejected only from our side because of our unbelief.

So here, Jesus declares the very heart of God over humanity in its most darkened state: "Father, forgive." It is a word of love that comes to the unlovable. It is a love that meets us in our lowest point, our sin. For the gospel to be what it is, it must be grounded in who God is in the essence of His person and revealed to us through Jesus, who was and is fully clothed in His own gospel. His forgiveness is an immovable reality grounded in His death and resurrection. His love and absolution can at times feel utterly elusive, but that doesn't make them any less real.

The Heart of the Heart

As the Lord has forgiven you, so you also must forgive.

—Colossians 3:13

As beautiful as forgiveness and reconciliation are, when it comes to God's call upon the forgiven to forgive others, it can feel impossible. Our identities often become wrapped up in the wrongs we have (or believe we have) endured. The natural inclination to sin means that bitterness and blame shifting are the repeated behaviors of our modern age—collectively and individually. As Jacques Ellul prophetically wrote in 1948 with such precision,

> Christians cannot consider themselves pure in comparison with others or declare themselves unaffected by the world's sin. A major fact of our civilization is that sin is becoming more and more collective, and each individual person is constrained to participate in it.*

*Jacques Ellul, *Presence in the Modern World,* trans. Lisa Richmond (Eugene, Ore.: Wipf and Stock, 2016), 5.

Our capacity for judgment toward others along with our simultaneous justification of ourselves is deeply troubling. It reduces us to nothing more than the effects of another's cause. We become what has been done to us. So busy nursing our wounds, we become blind to ways that we participate in the wounding, or propagate the wounding, or wound others from our woundedness. We cannot recognize how fundamentally broken we are without divine intervention; it really doesn't matter how much light there is if we are blind. We need new sight, but when we receive it, we are often horrified by what we find. It's much easier to suppress and exchange the truth for a lie than to come into the light. It's easier to create our scapegoats. It's easier to play the victim.

A few years back I asked my dad if he believed in hell, and I was totally surprised by his response but not his logic. With his usual slightly agitated, raspy nonchalance, he said, "Yeah, I believe in hell."

"Why?"

"Because I know so many people that should go there!"

"What about you?"

He looked at me incredulously and replied, "Joshua, I am a good person!"

We need to point to someone else to explain the scars we bear, the glitches in our psyches, the dysfunction in our relationships, and the challenges that continually creep into our day-to-day lives. We long to place ourselves on the right side of our individual histories. Our culture has taught us to romance the trauma because we love the drama.

This is at the heart of the opaque proclamation, "I am this way because . . ." It is the primordial word from the garden: "The woman whom you gave to be with me, she gave me fruit of the tree, and I ate."*

Deflection is an affront to the very foundation of the gospel because it refuses to give grace to others while abusing it for ourselves. Forgiveness cuts at the bitter core of victimhood, for it is the reminder that Jesus died for the victim and victimizer; we all will find ourselves in both roles—often at the same time. As René Girard stated with such urgency, "The time has come for us to forgive one another. If we wait any longer there will not be time enough."**

. . .

I have often fruitlessly demanded my father's acknowledgment that he abandoned me. But every time I have withheld my love and my forgiveness, I have discovered I cannot wound him without wounding myself. I cannot erase him without erasing myself. It has always been a fool's errand. Every time I have brought up Dad's absence, his response has been, "I am not going to apologize for how I raised you!"

"You didn't raise me."

"Joshua, when you call, I want to feel better, not worse."

*Genesis 3:12.

**René Girard, *The Scapegoat,* trans. Yvonne Freccero (Baltimore: Johns Hopkins University Press, 1986), 212.

"I'm sorry, Dad, but you cannot tell me you have no regrets!"

"Joshua, I love you, but I am not going to talk about this."

End of conversation.

My father's words, "You didn't want to be with me," that were spoken over me in that claustrophobic house of sadness led me to write this book. I am committed to looking for the pinpoints of grace in every story and not letting myself play the victim, but I also know how damaging it can be when we refuse to say, "What happened was not okay." When we get hung up on an event that haunts us, we need to let the Spirit of truth show us what might be hurting us—or worse, what is hurting others through us now. It's not simply insight I am after but the ability to truly forgive. Actually what I really want is healing, which includes both forgiveness and insight. It is not an exaggeration to say that every time I have wanted to abandon what feels like the impossible work of reconciliation with my father, I find myself confronted with words of Jesus on the cross and the divine mystery of His saving work. It might seem ludicrous to apologize to my dad for something that happened when I was two. For some it might seem like a willful refusal to hold him accountable for his abandonment of us boys and his absolute unwillingness to contribute to our upbringing, which left my mother with the emotional and financial burden. With Dad, there has never been even an openness to apologize. It would be dishonest to say that is not a hard pill to swallow, but the admonition of Scripture to honor our mother and father comes with no contingency.

Even more inescapable is the conviction of the Spirit that I cannot speak of my own absolution while refusing the same to those who have hurt me. *The forgiven must forgive,* as Jesus warned. Why? Because forgiveness removes barriers to love. I have never found it hard to forgive. Or so I thought, until I realized that my forgiveness for my father was in the abstract and amounted to nothing more than that evil sin of acedia, or indifference. I'm not one who holds on to things—that is, I am not easily offended, and I am grateful for that temperament. However, I must always ask, Have I really forgiven the person who has sinned against me? Or is it just a cover for the dark possibility that the person simply holds no significance in my life? Some people want to make the perpetrator pay. That is vengeance, which might be the lesser evil, for at least there is feeling rather than the cold belief in a false forgiveness, achieved by refusing to acknowledge that the person exists at all. This was the troubling revelation that broke through the hardness of my heart.*

There must be a *relational proximity* to the forgiven if the forgiveness is to be meaningful. It is not my mental release of wrongs, which someone may or may not be

*It's hard to admit that when I was a young adult, before meeting Jesus, as a way of protecting myself from people I perceived as threats, I lived by the unspoken maxim "You can't hurt me if I refuse your existence." What a horrific way to live, but even more troubling is that same maxim's ability to survive under the guise of a false forgiveness today.

aware of, that is needed but my love. A love that flows freely from one who has been forgiven much to the forgiven other. We need not concern ourselves with the other's response. We are not responsible for that, but as painful as a refusal to reconcile is, we must hold on to hope with a readiness to receive the offended.

We must let the forgiving Christ be responsible for us. It is His prerogative to forgive and to love through us. This is the only tangible evidence that the barriers are removed. This is the reason I stand firmly in the conviction that the loveless Christian is an illusion.

2.

The Cross of Division & Acceptance

The Second Word from the Cross

One of the criminals who were hanged railed at him, saying, "Are you not the Christ? Save yourself and us!" But the other rebuked him, saying, "Do you not fear God, since you are under the same sentence of condemnation? And we indeed justly, for we are receiving the due reward of our deeds; but this man has done nothing wrong." And he said, "Jesus, remember me when you come into your kingdom." And he said to him, "Truly, I say to you, today you will be with me in paradise."

—Luke 23:39–43

Drawn & Divided

And I, when I am lifted up from the earth,
will draw all people to myself.

—John 12:32

One cannot read the Gospels honestly and deny the magnetism present in the person of Jesus. The fact is this: People were drawn to Him then, and people are still drawn to Him today. This is the supernatural outworking of His own words, "And I, when I am lifted up from the earth, *will draw all* people to myself."*

Those beautiful words are neither hyperbolic nor some future promise of salvation for all (for all may be drawn, but the response is varied). The triumph of Spirit-filled witness will always carry with it the heartbreak of those who feel the pull but say no.

Even today, simply to mention His name seriously in a public setting will inevitably evoke a visceral response. I encountered this twenty-two years ago, contrarian that I

*John 12:32, emphasis added.

am, and it created an insatiable curiosity in me about the person of Jesus and ultimately led to my conversion. I just could not get my head around why my casual hedonistic acquaintances could be so provoked by a young man asking questions about a Jesus he didn't yet fully believe in.

I recall the first conversation in my "seeking" stage. It was with a group of friends and fellow musicians at the Crocodile, a music venue, in Seattle in 1999. We were having a relatively lively discussion about the books we were reading. I mentioned I had just finished the complete short stories of Kafka. A very charming, Cambridge-educated English singer-songwriter said, with his lovely accent that had the air of a condescending but pleasant professor, "I think Kafka is a very religious writer, interesting but exhausting. I'm afraid it's not my cup of tea."

I saw this as my opportunity to pose the question I was really thinking about. So I blurted out in nervous excitement, "I'm also reading the Bible for the first time. What do you guys think about Jesus?"

The Englishman was the only one smiling, and then he burst out laughing awkwardly. The rest of the table tried to laugh it off while simultaneously looking at me as if I had no clothes on and was about to attempt a group hug. Let me just say, the nervous discomfort was palpable.

I knew from that moment that there was power in the name of Jesus.

. . .

Nowhere is Jesus's ability to draw people in and divide them more easily observed than in the narratives around the crucifixion. The effect of the crucified God being lifted up polarizes as fully as it unites. There is either repentance and confession or hatred and contempt, belief and acceptance or unbelief and rejection. One thing is for certain: It is never neutral. This is why Jesus will go down in history as the most loved and hated individual who has ever lived. Here we have Jesus lifted up from the earth, and people are drawn to Him, but the response is division. This picture is painted for us perfectly in the second word of the crucified King. Two nameless criminals were crucified, one on each side of Him. Both were being drawn to Jesus, but their responses reveal that the sword of Christ divides. Both asked for salvation, but one man's animus and unrepentant demand became a wall of separation, while the other man's humble request became a door of hope.

Your Old Man Was Just Having Fun

[1980]

All forgiveness is suffering.

—**Dietrich Bonhoeffer**

The orange-and-cream 1969 F-100 swerved as my dad reached around the floor for another Oly from the half rack at his feet. He tossed one to me over my five-year-old brother, who sat between us on the worn bench seat.

"Go ahead, Joshua, but you better not go tellin' your mom! You hear me?"

To my seven-year-old palate, the lukewarm beer tasted bitter but pleasant; maybe I enjoyed that this drink was forbidden or that it was being shared with my dad—that mysterious man behind the wheel, long dirty-blond hair pulled back into a ponytail, flannel shirt rolled up, wearing Wranglers and boots. He was gruff but not cruel, twenty-seven but already worn, handsome like Cobain, always unkempt, never without a Camel cigarette hanging from his lips, and rarely without a beer or whiskey in hand.

It was the summer. Mom had given Dad permission to take us boys to his farmhouse for two weeks, outside of Omak along the Okanogan River in northern Washington. He decided to keep us for a month, which, combined with the discovery of his drug use, solidified my mother's refusal to let us stay with him for the next five years.

That summer trip to my father's place was marked primarily by his absence, or perhaps by my invisibility. I remember his birthday, which falls in late June, because I walked into the dim living room without anyone noticing just after my dad had opened his birthday gift from Big Bob, a towering, bearded biker with a single thick braid that went to the middle of his Harley leather vest. Bob had a booming laugh and eyes that were simultaneously kind and dangerous. The birthday gift was an ivory straw, which my father was using to snort a line of cocaine off a mirror that had an image of a naked woman on it.

Everyone watched Dad entranced, with hungry noses, as I innocently walked up to the table and asked him what the gift was. I'll never forget his response as he looked up with wild eyes and slight agitation: "Joshua, what the hell are you doing in here? Go outside."

"But what is it?"

"This is a special straw that your dad uses to take his nose medicine."

Everyone laughed.

"What's your nose medicine for? Are you okay, Dad?" I asked with nervous concern.

"Joshua, I'm fine. Stop asking so many questions. Now go outside and play with your brother!"

As the screen door closed behind me, I heard faint laughter from behind, and I didn't understand why I felt so small and embarrassed. I wished for the moment I could go home, but to what?

I had nowhere to go, and so I cried.

. . .

Years later, I called Dad to ask about this incident while he was in a rehabilitation center in Anchorage, Alaska. He had not drunk or smoked since Christmas. He was clear and feisty. He laughed and said, "You were pretty sensitive, and your mom overreacted."

When I asked him about the cocaine, he said, "Your old man was just having fun. Maybe a little too much fun."

It was amazing to hear such fond nostalgia in his voice. "Dad, you were selling cocaine!"

He interrupted me: "Remember on that trip when I took you fishing, we caught so many trout? I loved having you boys with me. I remember when Binx and Big Bob came to the house with two half racks in the middle of the night. They kicked the front door in and plopped down on the couch. I came out of my room half-asleep, in my underwear, with my revolver in hand ready to shoot. Yeah, those were good days . . ."

. . .

My life has been haunted by my father's absence and often tormented by his presence. I have barely known him, but somehow, we know each other. He never chose me or my brother—although he would never admit that, and I am sure he does not believe it. I have come to the conclusion that something broken and buried deep within his constitution made that choice an impossibility. But then again, I have for much of my life repeated the same pattern—choosing to return the unchoice.

How could a man I did not grow up with imprint so much of his temperament upon my soul? I can't escape seeing my face in his, no matter how weathered or worn-out it is, nor do I want to. Here in his tired twilight, we have discovered our need for each other. He didn't choose me, but I know he loves me in his own broken way, and I him.

Forgiveness has taken root and the barriers between us have begun to fall as relational proximity increases. The Founder and Finisher of faith has begun to lay a foundation for Dad and me. I can feel it being played out even in our dysfunctional exchanges. He has chosen to bring us together. He has chosen me to be one of the conduits of grace by which He is pursuing my father all the way to the grave. He is patient because the victory is already won, but it takes time, time for me to be transformed by His finished work and time for my dad to respond to the love that chooses him where he is. Jesus reminds me again and again, through this seemingly impossible relationship, that faith in Him must include faith for my father. I can't say I love Jesus and place my hope in Him and not extend the same hope to my dad, Alexander.

. . .

I am so grateful for the care and patience of Jesus, yet for me it's not fast enough. The impulsive and anxious side of me finds the wait unbearable. Every time I receive a call from the hospital, I think it's too late. This leads to a collapse in faith as I fall back on seeking to persuade my dad lovelessly, devoid of the Spirit. This is as futile as it is sinful. It is strange how fear often manifests in anger and impatience. I'll call Dad and say, "Dad, I don't understand why you won't just surrender to Jesus. Don't you understand you're dying? Don't you understand you don't have anything to offer Him other than your dirty old curmudgeon self?"

Thus begins the loop, for the impatience and coldness in my fear exasperates my father, who is terrified of dying (which is the primary reason he drinks). It is his double bind. This line of questioning usually ends with my father, a man of few words, suddenly throwing down a quick succession of words. If Scrabble were played using only expletives, my father would be a world champion.

What is most heartbreaking about my approach—and I am recognizing it only as I read through these words—is that it reduces my father to an inconvenient project rather than someone wholly loved and patiently pursued by God. It also reveals the ease at which we can enter into the service of others with a bitter spirit. We become martyrs in the modern sense of the word, making sure everyone knows how much we sacrifice while hiding the fact that we are devoid of love. The problem is that we, like the first thief, do not understand that Christ can give us nothing separated from Himself. He is the giver and the gift. He is the one building through us, even in spite of us.

The last time I asked my dad why he wouldn't surrender, I felt the Spirit ask me the same question.

Forgive me, Lord.

The Shadow Man & the Beautiful Exchange

> Every one of us is shadowed by an illusory person:
> a false self. This is the man that I want myself to be
> but who cannot exist, because God does not know
> anything about him. And to be unknown of God
> is altogether too much privacy.

—Thomas Merton, *New Seeds of Contemplation*

Nonbeing is a word that can threaten us and make our blood go cold. Yet in my own history, it has not been the inescapable reality of death that has brought the terror of that repugnant word into view. When I was young, the threat came in the form of loneliness. Due to endless uprooting, I always sat on the outside of the social order—invisible. It was as if the world refused to acknowledge that I existed.* To be honest, I sometimes wondered if I did. As sad as that is, what troubles me more are those seasons of self-inflicted isolation that, as an adult, have

---

*To what extent that was true I can't say, for such is the nature of memory and its ability to grow to mythological proportions over time. However, myths do carry a germ of truth as well as provide us with archetypes of the human experience.

threatened me with such existential dread and hopeless-
ness that life itself became unbearable to live. How can
one choose the shadow self and it be any other way? This
is the essence of sin; it is the active nothingness of the
selfish self that enslaves, isolates, and brings forth death.
To "be" demands knowing and being known, if life is to
be meaningful. I am because you are. More importantly,
we are because God is a community within Himself.

. . .

The first thief demanded rescue from Jesus while simultaneously rejecting Him. Listen to the subtle mockery in his
words: "One of the criminals who were hanged railed at
him, saying, 'Are you not the Christ? Save yourself and
us!' "*

The silence of Jesus toward the first thief is not indifference. God's love for this man cannot be less than it is for
the other. To qualify that statement—His love for sinful
humanity is aimed at setting us free. From what? From
our false selves so that we might become what He intended. But He cannot love what is not true. The shadow
self is the outcome of the hell-bent belief that we are the
masters of our own lives. The first thief rejected the God-
man by refusing to surrender to the light. He hung helplessly with the shadow of death over him, and yet he
refused to believe he wasn't free. He would not accept

*Luke 23:39.

that he had become a phantom, a shadow of what the crucified King intended. He hangs in history as a heart-breaking reminder that there will always be people who prefer the dark over the light of Christ. The "thy will" of Jesus is rejected for the "I will" of the ruler of this world, Satan. The Father of Lies has come to give us death and give it to us abundantly. As long as we hold stubbornly to the false selves of our own making, we remain strangers to God. As Thomas Merton stated, "God does not know anything about him." Jesus declared in the Sermon on the Mount,

> Not everyone who says to me, "Lord, Lord," will enter the kingdom of heaven, but the one who does the will of my Father who is in heaven. On that day many will say to me, "Lord, Lord, did we not prophesy in your name, and cast out demons in your name, and do many mighty works in your name?" And then will I declare to them, "I never knew you; depart from me, you workers of lawlessness."*

This should be a warning to all who call Jesus "Lord." The first thief did not use this title, which makes him possibly more honest than the people in the pew who live under the illusion that their obedience to a Jesus they have never known makes them Christians. The replacement of sur-

*Matthew 7:21–23.

render and relationship with behavior modification will always be a problem in the church. Jesus was continually addressing it two thousand years ago, and He still is today. When Jesus says, "I never knew you," this is not a statement of cruel rejection or ignorance but the One who is the truth declaring (I am sure with heartbreak), "I do not know the 'you' you chose to be!" Why? Because he or she does not exist in the light but in the world of darkness and illusion.

. . .

In contrast to the first thief, the absolution and acceptance of the second thief into the kingdom of God is a reminder of just how alien the economy of grace is to the modern mind. Even more difficult is holding in tension the story's historicity with the cosmic and transcendent nature of the crucified Christ and His promise of freedom proclaimed over a lost sinner. As George MacDonald wrote:

> Christ is the way out, and the way in; the way from slavery, conscious or unconscious, into liberty; the way from the unhomeliness of things to the home we desire but do not know; the way from the stormy skirts of the Father's garments to the peace of His bosom.*

*George MacDonald, *Unspoken Sermons* (New York: Cosimo, 2007), 247.

Though archetypal and symbolic, this story cannot be read as myth, for the life, death, and resurrection of Jesus the Son of God is inexorably anchored in our world's violent and bloody history. What happened in a particular moment in time continues to happen. It is the paragon of truth, *splendor sine occasu:*[*] God pursues and saves lost people. The thief found himself accepted by the crucified King. The threat of nonbeing was instantly annihilated by the Living Word's dying words, "Truly, I say to you, today you will be with me in paradise."[**]

The exchange is so intimate that the other players in the scene, and even the anguish of mental and physical torture, seem to fade from view. This sacred exchange between the crucified King and the thief was not delusional thinking brought on by acute suffering and the threat of nonexistence. Being tortured to death was never meant to bring people together; it was meant to isolate, humiliate, deconstruct, and ultimately end life while maximizing suffering.

At death's door the thief cast his hope on the One whose innocence and compassion could not be extinguished by the cross. What was he really asking Jesus for? Did he believe in life after death for himself? He did for Jesus. Humanity has always been haunted by a sense that we are meant for more. He clearly saw the "more" in the One who was dying next to him. This is obvious in his

[*]Splendor without diminishment.
[**]Luke 23:43.

rebuke of the other thief, "Do you not fear God, since you are under the same sentence of condemnation? And we indeed justly, for we are receiving the due reward of our deeds; but this man has done nothing wrong."*

The miraculous shift in this man's treatment of Jesus reminds us of the power of the cross to draw the godless to the forsaken God. The gospel of Matthew states that this man railed against Jesus with the other thief.** But what began with blind accusation ended in belief and acceptance. The darkness of that hour could not prevent the light of Jesus from revealing the reality of who He is and what the thief was without Him. A merging of the fear of God, which is the beginning of wisdom, with the innocence of the crucified Christ drew from the thief's suffering lips that statement of childlike faith, "Jesus, remember me when you come into your kingdom."***

The thief called Him "Jesus," not "Lord." He used the human name when addressing his Savior. This wasn't done in irreverence—in fact, "Lord" is assumed in his acknowledgment that the kingdom belongs to Jesus. The familiarity of his address is the outcome of the Spirit drawing him into the light, where his request is the "yes" of faith to the simultaneous "yes" and "no" of God. His explicit faith in Jesus meant that he surrendered to God's "no," that is, judgment on his sin, and accepted his place in

*Luke 23:40–41.

**See Matthew 27:44.

***Luke 23:42.

God's kingdom, God's "yes." His apprehension became revelation in the presence of the humble King who closed the conversation with a promise of transformation. Jesus responded with the same familiarity and more grace, "Truly, I say to you, today you will be with me in paradise."*

I Like Your Boots

[2012]

What is grace? Grace is love that seeks you out when you have nothing to give in return. Grace is love coming at you that has nothing to do with you. Grace is being loved when you are unlovable. It is being loved when you are the opposite of loveable.

—**Paul Zahl,** *Grace in Practice*

We were driving down Martin Luther King Jr. Boulevard. It was a fall day, and the trees were beginning to turn. I was out on a date with little Miss Hattie, my five-year-old. At that age she had an unshakable internal will. Combined with her indomitable dynamism, that meant that whether loving or lamenting, she always gave 100 percent.

Her eyes, like mine, are large, but she and her brother have the cerulean blue irises of their mother—eyes that seem flecked with light itself. Those irises push out to their blue-gray limbal rings, which seem to keep the light from escaping their faces. At five, her face had not yet caught up with those radiant disks and, unlike Henry and Darcy, who have a calming effect when they look at you, that light-filled blue has always carried a certain wildness in Hattie, which matches what's going on inside her giant heart.

She was sitting in her car seat in our 1987 blue Volvo Station Wagon when I glanced in the mirror at her. Her eyes told me before words flew that she was about to drop some knowledge (whether I was asking for it or not): "Daddy, I love Grandpa and can't wait to meet him!"

The sheer directness of the statement provoked in me a response that could not be called pastoral or fatherly, and I still cringe even as I write it down. I had just begun to engage with my father after five years of radio silence. I had bought him a ticket to fly down to meet his grandkids and so that I could get to know this man who had always been such an enigma to me. He was a source of much stress and, I am sad to say, embarrassment as well, due to his addictions and general lack of self-care. Overwhelmed by my own baggage, I lashed out at her undeterred affection, which to me felt inappropriate and over-blown. "Hattie, you can't say that. You haven't even met him. How can you love someone you haven't even met? You don't even know if he's a good person."

She replied without even picking up on my incredulity, "I love him because he's my grandpa and because he's your dad!"

She was done speaking and began to sing one of the many songs she had written without knowing how to play an instrument. As I thought about what she said, I was struck by the purity of her heart, the fierceness in her eyes, and the words of Scripture,

> Out of the mouth of babies and infants,
> you have established strength because of your
>   foes,
> to still the enemy and the avenger.*

This was a reminder of the divine qualities of childlikeness and the definition of love itself: "Love bears all things, believes all things, hopes all things, endures all things."**

. . .

The day I picked him up at the airport, I was shocked by how fragile he had become. I had not laid eyes on him in nine years, and time had not been kind. I retract that: Time had done nothing to him—it was he that had not taken time seriously and had abused his place in it. He was in a wheelchair being pushed toward me. He had a small, stained powder-gray 1980s duffel bag in his lap, Camel Reds sticking out of his oversized T-shirt pocket, and an unlit cigarette

*Psalm 8:2.

**1 Corinthians 13:7.

hanging from his tense lips. He was berating the poor airport employee for moving too slow and not taking his need to smoke with the same degree of seriousness that he did. I apologized to the young man and took over, only to be met with the same distress and frustration.

That scowling face was like a more haggard version of Willie Nelson. His hair was gray, long, and greasy under a filthy trucker hat. He wore dirty gray sweats that were tight at the bottom. His untied no-brand tennis shoes with holes met his naked ankles, translucent and hairless. We got in the car after he smoked. I wouldn't let him smoke inside, so he made me pull over every fifteen minutes of the two-and-a-half-hour drive from Seattle to Portland. At my request, we stopped at my little brother's place in West Seattle so Dad could shower. He came out in Wranglers, his cowboy boots, and the new trucker hat I had bought him at breakfast and insisted he wear.

I could not figure out what had happened to him. I knew he was nervous to meet the kids, but his breathing was shallow, and he still hadn't told me why he was using a walker. I probed (much to his irritation), and after a few minutes and a couple of mini bottles of vodka, he confessed he had suffered at least two strokes that year, which had left him struggling to walk, his right arm weak, and his mind a bit fragmented.

I had warned the kids about my father's smoking and drinking, and I had specifically asked Hattie to *please* not bring up Grandpa's smoking with him. I don't know where she got it, but she has a strange aversion to cigarettes and, like her mother, has no problem confronting things she disagrees with. In that conversation, she quickly asked me, "Why does Grandpa smoke? Does he know smoking will kill him?"

"Yes, he does. And he does not care, so please don't ask, baby!"

"I won't, but he should know better!"

"He knows."

I had little confidence that she would hold up her end of the deal.

When we pulled up to the front of our house, I saw Hattie, who had been waiting for over half an hour on the front porch for our arrival, run down the sidewalk and open the car door for a man that she loved but had never met. "Hi, Grandpa. Can I help you into the house?"

She stuck out her little hand, and my dad gave her his. He replied with his deep, raspy voice, which hid his nervousness and undermined the emotion he was clearly experiencing, "Well, hello there, little lady!"

Dad swears to this day—a man who, until late, had no sensitivity to any kind of numinous experience—that when Hattie touched him, it was like energy entering his body. He was hooked, and since that visit, he has called her his "little lady," though he has only seen her twice.

I pulled the walker from the back of the Volvo, and Hattie walked alongside my dad, holding on to his arm as he slowly moved toward our front porch. At the steps, he looked down at her and said, "Little lady, Grandpa needs to have a smoke."

Darcy had come outside to stand on the porch. Her beauty and calming demeanor, combined with the unquestioning yet inquisitive love of Hattie, were clearly shaking my father to the core. He could barely stand having two sets of those cerulean eyes shining a light on him. Yet at the same time he looked like he couldn't bear the idea of them not being there to let him know he was seen, loved, and *accepted*. It was a strange thing to watch my dad's turmoil—he simultaneously looked like he would like to hide and never leave at the same time. Such is the nature of coming into the light.

Hattie stood between us as my dad sat down on his walker and lit up his cigarette. I peered down at Hattie and watched her eyes move from my father to his cigarette to my face and then back to my father. I was waiting for her bubble to burst when out of her mouth came these unadorned but earnest words: "I really like your boots, Grandpa!"

"Thank you, little lady. You are beautiful!"

"Thank you, Grandpa Al. I love you."

My dad was visibly moved. "I love you too, little lady!"

Like the thief, my dad received what he did not earn, and he could barely handle it. Hattie's unwavering love, a love without contingency, brought with it a kindness he was not accustomed to. I am sure it made him reflect on how fickle his affections, like mine, could be. He could have walked away—he probably thought about it—but instead he surrendered his will to her *acceptance* of him as he was and tasted *grace*. I could see the change in his sad eyes—they brightened. It made him, if only for a time, a better version of himself. It planted the seed within him that he could not shake and left him God-haunted. To be *accepted* is to receive *grace,* and *grace* is always unfair!

Speak It Out

Therefore, confess your sins to one another and pray for
one another, that you may be healed. The prayer of a
righteous person has great power as it is working.

—James 5:16

The cross of Christ is where sin, like death, has lost its
sting. Sin and death are defeated enemies.

But defeat doesn't mean sin does not remain a real and
dangerous foe. Yes, our sins have been forgiven and can
never be unforgiven.* But they can still bring much pain
and destruction to our lives. Victory for the believer is the
sinlessness of the Son as our new identity. That does not
mean we do not sin. Sin may be defeated and forgiven,
but we must still confront it and confess it, not only to
God but also to one another.

The thief's rebuke of the other thief is his own confession of their shared guilt. It is his repentance and his freedom, not from the earthly consequences, for his death on

---

*"Forgiven sin can, of course, still continue in all its guilt and corruption, but it can-
not again become sin unforgiven and triumphant." Karl Barth, *Church Dogmatics:
The Doctrine of the Word of God,* vol. 1.2 (London: Bloomsbury, 2004), 433.

the cross is a harsh reminder of the law of cause and effect. It is the overriding of an eternal separation and the healing of relationship between God and humanity. It has been said that death for the believer is how we will be ushered into more life. The same can be said of sin. Our sin may be forgiven, but if we hide it, it hides God from our senses. Confession is our acceptance of the forgiveness that is already ours. This is why sin confessed is often the place in which He, the forgiving God, meets us most powerfully and intimately.

There is renewed interest in the church today about spiritual disciplines, especially the contemplative practices of silence and solitude. But as wonderful as those are in their proper context, what is needed in the church today more than ever is a return to the discipline of honest confession.

When it comes to forgiveness, silence will benefit no one who is suffocating under the crushing weight of unconfessed sin. Learning to be alone with our thoughts may be necessary in this age of noise and spectacle, but how can it benefit us if we do not know how to share our burdens with one another?

If we are weak on confession or witness, does not solitude just become another way to stay in hiding? If we are made in the image of a triune God who is a community within Himself, then it is fair to say His image in us is *relational*. This is why God declared over humanity a statement we will consider in greater depth in chapter 4: "It is not good for the man to be alone."*

*Genesis 2:18, NIV.

It may be true that we should be slow to speak. But it is also true that we should be quick to confess, quick to forgive, and quick to share Jesus. The world is not compelled by our pretense or our silence but by our radical vulnerability—our honesty about our sin and our loving witness to the King who has forgiven us.

Sin leaves the body, *salvation* enters the soul, and *Jesus* is introduced by the mouth.

We must learn, slowly, to tell the truth.

When Thieves
Become Sheep

The saying is trustworthy and deserving of full
acceptance, that Christ Jesus came into the world to
save sinners, of whom I am the foremost.

—1 Timothy 1:15

"Thief" and "criminal" are the only identifiers given to
this man. His existence before Jesus had been reduced to
his worst acts. From his own confession, those acts may
have defined him appropriately.

In the gospel of John, Jesus spoke metaphorically of
His followers as sheep and Himself as both the "door" by
which the sheep enter and the "good shepherd" who lays
down His life for them.* He declared that they would
know His voice and follow Him. There is one verse from
this passage that kept coming to mind as I meditated on
this interaction from the cross: "The thief comes only to

*See John 10:1–18.

steal and kill and destroy. I came that they may have life and have it abundantly."*

This nameless man was being executed for stealing and most likely for killing as well. Such is the destructive nature of sin. Who, then, is the "they" that Jesus came to give life to? Is it not appropriate to say the sheep? Yes, but how can He not be referring to thieves as well? We shouldn't forget it's not sheep we are talking about but people. What kind of people? The only kind that exist: Sinful people. Our metaphor may be closer to a fairy tale, for though not all thieves become sheep, there is not a sheep in the fold who wasn't at one time a thief. Even more baffling is the destruction sheep can cause, even under the care of the Good Shepherd, because of their mixture of sin and righteousness. In fact, as a shepherd of a flock I have come to the conclusion that wolves—though potentially deadly and always damaging—are more often than not sheep.

Scripture declares with repeated force that murderers, adulterers, liars, idolaters, and the sexually immoral (and this list is by no means exhaustive) shall not inherit the kingdom of heaven. Yet apart from God and His angels, those are the only people who are invited in and the only people who are there because that's the only kind of people there are! How can that be? It is the golden chain: Jesus is lifted up and people are drawn; as they are drawn, they are exposed; as they are exposed, they repent and

*John 10:10.

surrender to His acceptance. Accepted, they receive the very Spirit of the sinless Christ in them. Now hidden in Christ, they are sinners forgiven despite their sin. New identity, new presence, new power, new purpose, new family, new destination—all are now present in the context of the same old sinner.

So yes, while it's true a murderer may not inherit the kingdom of God, there will also not be anyone who inherits that kingdom who is not a murderer. The difference is that one accepted the "yes" of Jesus, with an *active passivity* (one of those beautiful paradoxes in the gospel, where our work is our faith in Jesus who has worked out our salvation*), saying, "Yes, Lord, I receive." The other rejected the "yes" of Jesus, choosing the unchoice.** The "no" is not explicit but is found in his *active futility*. That is, his life was controlled by "I will!" That is a life of disconnect from the source of life, light, and truth—God

---

*John 6:29, "Jesus answered them, 'This is the work of God, that you believe in him whom he has sent.' "

**I have personally been helped and baffled by the dialectical approach that Karl Barth took in his *Church Dogmatics*. He defined *evil* by stating, "Evil in the first instance is . . . what God does not will." He referred to this as *das Nichtige:* "The nothingness" or "the impossible possibility." Karl Barth, *Church Dogmatics: The Doctrine of Reconciliation,* vol. 4.3.1 (London: Bloomsbury, 2004), 177, 178.

He wrote, "When I speak of nothingness, I cannot mean that evil is nothing, that it does not exist, or that it has no reality. . . . It does not exist as God does, nor as His creatures, amongst which it is not to be numbered. It has no basis for its being. It has no right to the existence which to our sorrow we cannot deny to it. Its existence, significance and reality are not distinguished by any value nor positive strength." Barth, *Church Dogmatics,* vol. 4.3.1, 178.

His argument, though dense, as I understand it, is simply that God is light and in Him there is no darkness (i.e., evil). Therefore, evil cannot have its origin in God, the source of all being, and must ultimately come to absolute nothing (an end) because whatever it is or isn't, it has been defeated by the victory of Jesus.

Himself. That is to choose a reality for ourselves that has no real substance and yet has concrete consequences in God's creation. To live the lie "I am my own god" is to choose a choice that has no basis for being and is in direct opposition to God, so it must ultimately come to nothing.

3.

The Cross of Heartbreak & Comfort

The Third Word from the Cross

But standing by the cross of Jesus were his mother and his mother's sister, Mary the wife of Clopas, and Mary Magdalene. When Jesus saw his mother and the disciple whom he loved standing nearby, he said to his mother, "Woman, behold, your son!" Then he said to the disciple, "Behold, your mother!" And from that hour the disciple took her to his own home.

—John 19:25–27

The Sword in Her Heart

I shall look at the world through tears. Perhaps I shall
see things that dry-eyed I could not see.

—Nicholas Wolterstorff, *Lament for a Son*

It's difficult to enter into another's pain, but we must try if
we are to understand the third statement from the cross.
Here we find the absolute helplessness and anguish of a
mother standing before her suffering and crucified son.
Like the thieves on the cross, she had no control over her
situation.

Here He was, her firstborn of miraculous conception.
She had been selected and blessed by God as the one
who would carry and give birth to Israel's hope, the Messiah. The prophetic word spoken to her was now being
fulfilled before her eyes. The sword that would pierce her
heart was striking its mortal blow.

What she could not have understood in the anguished
silence before the cross was that her messianic hope in
her firstborn, who was now writhing in incomprehensible
anguish before her eyes, had been misguided. As with His

disciples and the rest of Israel, her vision had been too narrow.* Yes, He was Israel's Messiah, but God elected Israel from among the nations so that they might be a conduit of His manifest presence and grace to the very nations they had been separated from.** He is the Savior of the world, and His revolution—which would not be understood until after Pentecost—would come through the cross she now stood before, not by the sword.

The death of Mary's dreams for her firstborn was not the end of the story but only the beginning. For in His words of compassion, He showed His concern for both the physical and the spiritual needs of this lovely woman.

. . .

Every parent has dreams for their children. Crucifixion is not one of them.

But through Mary's crushing loss, she received a new son, a new home, and (most importantly) a Savior who would transfer His Sonship to her and soon make His home within her! She thought she had lost Him. What she didn't know was she, like the rest of us, was being found.

---

*I say this with absolute reverence for Mary's unique role in human history, her beautiful faith, and her courage to endure all that she did through the thirty-three years of life she experienced as Jesus's mother.

**Exodus 19:5–6.

SIXTH FRAGMENT

I Am with You

[1979]

There is peace and rest and comfort in sorrow.

—Søren Kierkegaard, *Fear and Trembling*

My mom married my first stand-in dad when I was six. He was a consummate philanderer who lived with his two daughters in a single-wide trailer that rested at the base of the Lewis and Clark Bridge in the small town of Rainier, Oregon. At the time of its completion in 1930, it was the largest cantilever bridge in America. It crossed the Columbia River and connected Washington and Oregon, as well as the two towns I moved back and forth between like a yo-yo for most of my childhood.

Our trailer faced a giant field that was meticulously cared for and guarded with a shotgun from subterranean dwellers—remember the mole?—by my stepdad's grandfather. He was an old-timer who lived in another house on the property. He sold earthworms and the whirligigs he made, which hung from his front porch, hypnotically spinning in the wind off the Columbia River. The memories of my time outside in that yard and the connecting fields feel far more visceral and open than the compressed and shrouded details within the trailer. The recollections flow unrestrained of times that were, most notably, unsupervised: If it was not raining, all play was outside and free from adults—with the exception of the old man, but his awareness of us was seemingly nonexistent.

A lifetime seems compressed into those two years. This was the place where we picked blackberries for cobbler, caught bees in cups turned upside down, and caught salamanders—who sometimes released their tails for escape—under the rocks, at the edge of the field, in the moist dirt, and in the shadow of the bridge. It is here I learned to ride a bike alone, coasting down the western slope with the bridge behind and crashing over and over in the soft grass until I didn't. It was here we—filled with excitement and fear—watched Mount Saint Helens blow. It was here my innocence was stolen at the hands of a stepsister I loved. Five years older than I, she drew my confused six-year-old body into her forbidden embrace and betrayed me with a kiss, repeating, I'm sure, things done to her in the shadows. I was ignored or harassed by a stand-in dad who terrified me. I was afraid of the dark, friendless, and insecure.

Yet nothing from all that time is etched in my memory like the comforting words and presence of my heartbroken mother the night she left that man and led my brother and I by the hands across the bridge toward a temporary freedom.

. . .

It was the witching hour. In the darkness of the claustrophobic hall just outside the bedroom where my brother and I were hiding under the bunk bed, my mom screamed at that spectral face who had broken her heart. He had been haunting some eighteen-year-old nymphet unbeknownst to my mom.

Yelling, scuffling, and a crash against the wall. The smell of fear was rising from our racing hearts in the dark of that room—so real I can taste its metallic presence even now as I write this thirty-nine years later. He had killed her. I just knew it. All had gone silent. I could not breathe. I couldn't survive without her. *Please, Mama, don't be dead. Please don't be dead!* My brother trembled in my arms. Time had been stilled. Each agonizing second was a lifetime lived, and I became ancient in a moment. As the door flew open, I closed my eyes, head bowed in existential dread.

"Joshua, Jarad, get dressed."

Mom. Beneath the moon, we moved through the

field. The warmth of my mother's hand and voice re-
assured us as we began our pilgrimage, walking
across the cantilever bridge. The inky river far below,
the narrow sidewalk, the creaking steel, the wind,
the shaking from the occasional semi carrying loads
of fresh-cut lumber, and the blinding headlights of
oncoming cars all reminded us that heaven and hell
hung in the balance. But as frightening as the journey seemed, I could not shake a strange sense of
peace, even joy, within the unknown of the night.
This was an exodus toward at least a momentary salvation. My mother spoke these comforting words:
"Don't be afraid. I am with you."

Across the bridge we left the yard, the trailer, the
girls, the grandpa, and the ghost of that man behind
us forever.

The Bread of Life & the Stone of Stumbling

Or which one of you, if his son asks him
for bread, will give him a stone?

—Matthew 7:9

Christianity's history has never been anchored in comfort. Its promise has never been a respite from our difficulty. We struggle with this because we are uncomfortable with paradox. How can the gospel, which means "good news," offer those who trust and follow Jesus things like joy, peace, and love with a caveat of heartache and suffering and still be truly good?

We have a knack for hearing what we want to hear and ignoring what is difficult. When the difficult comes, we are rarely prepared for it, and like so many that followed Jesus some two thousand years ago, we just stop following. His word, which once seemed so comforting, becomes too uncomfortable—it becomes difficult.

Remember, it was Jesus, the night of His betrayal in the secrecy of the upper room, who offered His disciples promise after glorious promise. But toward the close of that profound discourse, He casually tossed a rock into the basket of the bread. What? Jesus, at the beginning of His ministry, said something to the effect of, "What kind of person gives a kid a rock when they ask for bread?" And yet, after promising peace to His fearful followers, He immediately said in no uncertain terms to those who had left all to be with Him: "I have said these things to you, that in me you may have peace. In the world you will have tribulation. But take heart; I have overcome the world."*

The truth lies not in the separation of peace and tribulation, bread and rock, but in their coexistence. It is Jesus who is Himself our *peace* in the difficulty. It is Jesus who is at once the bread of life and the stone of stumbling. Do not be afraid of the stumbling bit. We only stumble because, in a world of ever-shifting ideologies, we are not accustomed to walking on such solid ground. We love and are loved in the hurt. We are comforted while we struggle and struggle while bringing comfort; it is the impossible nature of life colliding with the saving goodness of God. As the Scriptures declare,

> Praise be to the God and Father of our Lord
> Jesus Christ, the Father of compassion and the
> God of all comfort, who comforts us in all our
> troubles, so that we can comfort those in any

*John 16:33.

trouble with the comfort we ourselves receive from God.*

Like Mary, we must learn the hard lesson that our comfort is found in the struggle if we are to bring that same comfort to those who are hurting around us. Faith may be personal, but it is never private. God is present when we move toward one another, but if we look away from one another, we ignore Him. Life with and poured out for God and others is good, but it is not easy. It is beautiful, but costly—too costly for many. I am guilty as charged.

. . .

If we were to look through the history of the church, those who have experienced the presence of God most fully were not those who lived in isolation as means of escaping humanity. Rather, they were those more practical mystics who entered willingly into the world's pain as His witnesses. These are the ones that found something worth dying for—and die they often did. Their lives of intimacy and purpose illustrate what Isaiah called "the treasures of darkness."**

If the path of Jesus is outward and downward, then the strange result of refusing that path is a deformed, ingrown, and truncated gospel that cries out, "We want you, Jesus.

*2 Corinthians 1:3–4, NIV.

**Isaiah 45:3.

Fill us. Holy Spirit, meet us in this place. God, heal us, speak to us—but please don't send us, don't embarrass us. Love us, but please don't cause us pain."

. . .

Mary's comfort would come through her unwillingness to look away from Jesus's suffering. He was both her heartbreak and her hope in this mysterious exchange. Her courage before the impenetrable meaning of His suffering, especially in light of the disciples' fear and absence at the cross, is a picture of a beautiful faith and fierce love hoping in the dark. It is also a picture of unbearable loss and heartbreak. This is the death of dreams. She was blessed among women. Angels, Magi, holy men, simple shepherds, and a prophetess all confirmed that she was the mother of the Messiah. She had seen His miracles, she had heard His teachings, she had hidden it all in her heart and pondered the details of His miraculous life, and now for what? For here she stood helplessly staring at a Savior who, in that moment, was incapable of saving and at a son incapable of surviving. She had to have asked, "Is this what it means to be blessed?"

As we explore the death of dreams in greater depth, it is important to hold on to the good we've experienced no matter how painful the loss is. Nothing compares to the loss of someone loved, especially a child. No parent should outlive their children, and yet so many parents do. Both my mother-in-law, Mimi, and my Nana lost their only sons. Mimi lost Jason at twenty-three to AIDS, and Nana lost Jimmy at twenty-six when he was hit by a car while pumping gas. It changes everything. As Nicholas Wolterstorff, in *Lament for a Son,* wrote with such focused grief that it made me feel his loss, "When we gather now there's always someone missing, his absence as present as our presence, his silence as loud as our speech."*

As a pastor I have walked people through the process of grief after a major loss. Those that come out the other side with faith, hope, and love still intact are those who allow themselves the space to truly grieve without surrendering hope or losing the joy and love they had experienced with the one who is now gone. However, grief is so powerful that I have also witnessed it consume the one mourning so fully that their loss replaced the one they lost. Grief personified is a selfish companion.

. . .

We now must take into consideration the death of our dreams on a much broader level because there is much in life that can bring both joy and unbelievable heartache. Jesus uses all of it. We must remember that His primary goal is not to make us comfortable but to bring His

*Nicholas Wolterstorff, *Lament for a Son* (Grand Rapids, Mich.: Eerdmans, 1987), 14. If you have lost someone you love, I cannot recommend this book enough. The heartbreak is palpable, but so is the hope.

saving life into our lives by His Spirit. This is the good death and the source of comfort in the struggle. He is the bread and the stone. He, by His Spirit within us, is Himself the bread that nourishes our identity *in Him* and the stone our idols are smashed upon.

The Song That Made the Young Girls Cry

[1984]

Let me not wander in a barren dream,
But when I am consumed in the fire,
Give me new Phoenix wings to fly at my desire.

—John Keats, "On Sitting Down to Read King Lear Once Again"

The pastor's wife sat before me at the Hammond C3 organ in permed silver hair and a polyester dress. Her arms were flying as her short fingers worked the two-tiered keyboard and her orthopedic shoes stomped out the bass notes. The sincerity of the performance, somberness of the moment, and general lack of aesthetic sensibility created a strange and hypnotic appeal to her choppy rendition of Horatio Spafford's "It Is Well with My Soul."

I, the interloper, sat next to my mother in that grief-saturated sanctuary. The room was filled with tears and an orange-and-amber haze from the stained-glass windows common to small churches built across America in the fifties and sixties. My eleven-year-old hands were clammy as I looked to center stage where the closed casket rested. It contained the body of a teenage boy whom I had never met. It's cringeworthy to confess that my nervousness was not over the death, for I had never been close to death and, to my knowledge, had never met the boy. No, I was nervous because my mother and I had been asked to sing at the funeral by the boy's father, and next to us there was a row of teenage girls who seemed pulled directly from a John Hughes film. The cause of death of this young, handsome football star was the kind of story traffic violation classes are made of—a party after a Friday night game, an early morning drive home on windy rural roads, both kids drunk, ending in a tree hugging that leaves one dead and the other (I can only imagine) permanently psychologically destroyed.

The pastor's eulogy, from what I can remember, was filled with pedestrian theology, the usual pithy phrases thrown out against the absurdity of the loss:

> "He was a kind young man, a good friend, and an even better son!"
> "The Lord gives, and the Lord takes away."
> "He is in a better place now."

We had been asked to sing that Nashville-produced 1983 Christian megahit "Friends" by the

poster child of eighties American evangelicalism su-
perstardom, Michael W. Smith.*

As the accompaniment tape began, I stood next
to my mom, petrified but determined, mic in my
hand. I had the lead. She had the harmony. My
voice, a silky tenor, began the opening line with
great delicacy. I looked up with growing confidence.

I'm not going to lie: I felt pretty good about my
appearance that day. I had just received my first
perm, giving me what I thought was a flair of Kirk
Cameron in *Growing Pains*. I had on my new gray
Bugle Boy slacks with matching suspenders and my
pink short-sleeve button-up shirt. As I hit the pre-
chorus, the bevy of beauties became emotionally
unhinged by what Luther (referring to music) called
the "mistress and governess of human emotions."**
I, a conduit of melody and word, had broken open
the heavens and the deep, and the world within that
room was suddenly flooded with weeping.

As the chorus landed, I remember an overwhelming sensation as I looked at the melancholy eyes and
moist cheeks of those magical creatures in the front
row. They all radiated such longing that it was as if
we had become tethered together, and I believed my

*Affectionately known as "Smitty" by his most serious fans.

**Martin Luther, "Preface to Georg Rhau's Symphoniae iucundae (1538)," *Lu-
ther's Works: Liturgy and Hymns,* vol. 53 (Philadelphia: Fortress, 1957), 321.

prepubescent voice, in a small way, had become a spiritual guide through their dark night of the soul.

This is what I wanted to do with my life. My calling had come. I knew what I had to do. In the words of the great Barry Manilow (who came from a parallel universe to Smitty):

> I write the songs of love and special things
> I write the songs that make the young girls cry*

. . .

At the time it never occurred to me that the stares, the tears, the emotion of that funeral music was not for me but for the unseen boy who lay in the casket behind me. The song may have been a catalyst but not the cause.

How mysterious that an event can be experienced so differently but still shared nonetheless. Their grief, even if it was misunderstood, gave me a glimpse of hope, and my song, even if it wasn't the source of

---

*Barry Manilow's "I Write the Songs" from the album *Tryin' to Get the Feeling*, released in 1975, was a favorite of my mom's. My mom was a sucker for the saccharine soft rock of seventies music, and my early years were marked by a steady diet of artists like the Carpenters, Johnny Mathis, Bread, and Mr. Manilow, to name a few. My cool aunt intervened when I was in fourth grade and gave me my first two cassette tapes with Sugarhill Gang's "Rapper's Delight" and Michael Jackson's "Off the Wall," which opened a whole new universe to me. Unfortunately, it was too late to override the influence, for I might have been the only kid in my school that could perform "Can't Smile Without You" using only sign language and had every word of "Copacabana" memorized (which I have never forgotten).

the tears, gave them comfort and the space to release them.

This event birthed a lifelong pursuit of music that
has crushed and humiliated me as fully as it has
blessed me. Thank you, Smitty. Thank you for all
of it.*

*It is worth noting that I watched this man perform live in 1989 at Jesus
Northwest in a failed attempt to get a very cute Christian girl to date me.
Knowing my chances were slim, I had secretly digested a small piece of per-
forated blotter, which had the image of a small dancing test-tube man on it,
before leaving my house. Within forty-five minutes the LSD had completely
rewired my mode of perception. The Christian music festival became something more akin to a carnival filled with such outbursts of spiritual and patri-
otic zeal—both in sound and sight—that I was struck with a strange case of
holy laughter that plagued my whole day. I am sure this was more than a little off-putting to my love interest.

The Death of Dreams

In order to become myself I must cease to be what I always
thought I wanted to be, and in order to find myself I must
go out of myself, and in order to live I have to die.

—**Thomas Merton, *New Seeds of Contemplation***

When I began to write songs at age nineteen, I had a chorus of encouragers telling me that I had what it takes, and
I believed it. I moved to Seattle and pursued the dream
with a laser-like focus.

By twenty-one, I had a band that was quickly gaining a
following. By twenty-two, we had a record deal with a
major label. By twenty-three, we were opening shows for
bands that had achieved real fame, embraced and helped
by many of them. Then at twenty-four, the month before
Darcy and I were married, our album was finally released,
and the first single dropped on the radio that month. This
was it. Or so I thought.

I had met with the program director of 107.7 The End.
This was the station we needed behind us if we were
going to break beyond the Northwest, or so our label kept

telling us. It was one of three stations in the nineties referred to as the "tastemakers" or "gatekeepers." In those days, they defined what would be on the airwaves. The program director gushed, confirmed her love of the record and the single, and came to our show the next night (giving more hyperbolic praise afterward). But when our single dropped four days later, there was radio silence. Not one play.

Why? Because the song had been picked up a day early by a competitor station that did not have national prestige. The End refused to play it. I guess it would be more accurate to say the radio silenced us. We had somehow become a pawn in a silly rivalry between two stations, and that was it. The end. Two months later I was dropped by the label, married, and working for minimum wage at a record store that had a mural of my record painted on the side of it. Dreams die painfully.

But thankfully, that is not the end of the story. This was the crisis needed to birth in me a hunger for what I *actually* needed. For it was two years later, while reading the Bible, that I surrendered to the One whose grace met me with an all-consuming love. Still to this day (more than twenty-two years later), there are things that are dear to me that do not survive the consuming fire of that love. I've walked with Him long enough to trust Him with what He asks from me. However, that does not make the process of surrender less painful. I am reminded of these words, which I have memorized, written by George MacDonald from his *Unspoken Sermons:*

Nothing is inexorable but love. . . . For love loves
unto purity. Love has ever in view the absolute
loveliness of that which it beholds. Where loveliness is incomplete, and love cannot love its fill
of loving, it spends itself to make more lovely,
that it may love more; it strives for perfection,
even that itself may be perfected—not in itself,
but in the object. . . . Therefore, all that is not
beautiful in the beloved, all that comes between
and is not of love's kind, must be destroyed. And
our God is a consuming fire.*

. . .

The miraculous confirmation given to Mary—that she
had been chosen and blessed over all women to be the
mother of the world's Messiah—is what makes the scene
at the cross so unbearable. How many times must she
have asked, "Is this what it means to blessed?"

She was the mother of a son who would grow into a
man, hated as much as He was loved, misunderstood as
deeply as He was revered. But nothing could prepare her
for the One tortured beyond recognition in this scene. It
is hard to imagine the combination of helpless anguish
and internal disconnect that she must have experienced
as she stood before Him at the cross. This was death for
her on multiple levels: The death of a son, the death of a

*George MacDonald, *Unspoken Sermons* (New York: Cosimo, 2007), 24.

dream, and the death of a mother. She could not see the good and the promises that were coming through those agonizing deaths. In light of this I have never been comfortable with the statement, "God has a wonderful plan for your life."

It is not that the statement is untrue. It's that it is misleading. We are unable, at least in the West, to imagine unbearable suffering as a part of a wonderful plan. A better framework would be, "God has a perfect plan, but for you personally it might be quite difficult. It might even feel impossible."

But no matter how difficult, it must be simply stated that as His followers we are called to follow Him—who is our peace—not out to pasture but into His broken world.

The path of least resistance never produces the growth we want. There is no lasting comfort in the avoidance of pain. The challenge before us—dying with Him and letting Him lead—will always be harder than climbing our ladders. Why? Ladders create the illusion of control, courage, and strength. A ladder invites us to be active. Climbing feels better than losing control. Even falling feels better than being crucified. The gospel is down-to-earth, but that doesn't necessarily make us feel better—at least not at first because it requires an active passivity that feels somehow weak, even out of control.

The apostle Paul prayed for God to remove a "thorn" of suffering from his flesh. Paul did not disclose what the thorn was. It could have been spiritual, physical, psychological, or relational. But whatever it was, surely the answer that came was not what Paul wanted. God responded, "My grace is sufficient for you, for my power is made perfect in weakness."*

God is not here to plan our lives with us. He does not owe us an explanation of how His plan will be accomplished. In fact, He owes us nothing. We serve at the pleasure of the King, yet in His freedom He calls us to follow Him. Jesus never told His disciples where He was going; we need to remember that He is consistent. We can expect the same, not because He is being elusive but because it does not matter where we go as long as He's the one leading.

. . .

There is a mystery in human suffering that defies explanation. We can say that suffering has its root in sin, but that doesn't explain the dark intervals of loss and grief that existence carries with it. We may interpret God's involvement in suffering as indifference, allowance, or absence; if He is God, it is hard not to think of Him as involved. This is due to the limitations of our human perspective. We can spin our wheels trying futilely to understand why we suffer, or we can look upon the One who suffered with us and for us to find comfort and carry it to others. In the comforting words of Dorothy Sayers,

*2 Corinthians 12:9.

> For whatever reason God chose to make man as
> he is—limited and suffering and subject to sor-
> rows and death—He had the honesty and the
> courage to take His own medicine.*

We must remember, God can take the dissonant notes of our suffering and weave them into His redemptive song. What matters is not why I suffer. What matters is that God cares.

---

*Dorothy Sayers, *Creed or Chaos?* (San Diego: Harcourt, 1949), 4.

The Grain of Wheat

Truly, truly, I say to you, unless a grain of wheat
falls into the earth and dies, it remains alone;
but if it dies, it bears much fruit.

—John 12:24

When Jesus saw his mother and the disciple whom
he loved standing nearby, he said to his mother,
"Woman, behold, your son!" Then he said to the disciple,
"Behold, your mother!" And from that hour the
disciple took her to his own home.

—John 19:26–27

Mary, here at the close of this beautiful section, demonstrated a faith that worked by her full surrender to the
command and provision of the crucified Son who—
though she only understood it dimly—was her salvation.
His reference to her here, not as "mother" but "woman,"*
was not meant as insult but as reality. This was a final
severing of the mother-son relationship that had been

---

*This is the second recorded time that Jesus referred to His mother as "woman." The
first was also recorded in the gospel of John when He turned water into wine at
Mary's request (John 2:4).

strained since the beginning of His public ministry. Yes, she had the unique privilege of enjoying Him as her son, but now she had to die to that relationship. As impossibly painful as it was, it was the key to receiving what He was trying to give her. Even His provision of an earthly home with the apostle John pointed to something deeper still.

How hard it must have been to walk away from the One that came to her as a divine gift—the child she had nursed, raised, and protected. But her obedience here is consistent with her response to the angel Gabriel thirty-three years earlier. He declared that she was favored by God and chosen to carry the world's Messiah. Her response as a scared young woman—probably only about fifteen years of age—is one of the greatest statements of *surrendering faith* in Scripture: "Mary said, 'Behold, I am the servant of the Lord; let it be to me according to your word.' And the angel departed from her."*

She left Him alone. I'm sure it felt like a betrayal of every maternal instinct, but that was part of the *good death* occurring in her life. Jesus was not rejecting her as His earthly mother; He was receiving her as a sinner in need of a Savior. He was not interested in being her son— that wasn't what she needed—but in providing her with His Sonship. He gave her a physical home where she could lay her grieving head that night. But she would awake the next morning and, as is common for those who experience the devastation of death, have a blessed tem-

*Luke 1:38.

porary forgetfulness that dissipated as quickly as it was felt, leaving a suffocating void as her soul ached without respite. There were comforters there to comfort, but the anguish lay in the fact that she could no longer comfort Him any more than He could comfort her. Or so she thought.

. . .

There was a permanent home being built at the cross, a home that no one could understand. Human suffering would become the raw materials of its construction. Jesus, the architect of our faith, could only build it alone, hidden from our sight.

For on the cross, the forsaken God revealed that what looked like defeat was actually love triumphing over the cause of all human enslavement: Sin, the dominion of darkness, and the world's false systems. He did not simply dismantle the house of mirrors; He built Himself a new sanctuary, a new home that was guaranteed in His resurrection and actualized on Pentecost through His Spirit. Mary, like all who surrender to the crucified King, discovered Jesus was closer to her than He had ever been. She was a new creation, for she was now the dwelling place of the very One she had thought lost. Through His death and resurrection, He utilized the death of her dreams and the suffering of her life to build in her a *house of grace* by which He could permanently commune with her and bring comfort to others through her. One of the great principles of Scripture is that God places dreams in our hearts that must die before they can be brought to fruition. I have often said that at least in my own experience, God gives us what we want—in a way that we never could have imagined—only when we no longer need it. He said to His disciples the night of His betrayal, "If anyone loves me, he will keep my word, and my Father will love him, and we will come to him and make our home with him."*

. . .

I often find myself thinking back to the crossing of that bridge in the night. I remember the fear, the excitement, the heartbreak, and the comfort of my mom's words and warm hand leading us through the dark toward the dawning of a new morning. It's impossible not to view all the hurt, the poverty, the joy, and the love through the lens of the crucified King who spoke both comfort and challenge, "Behold, I am with you always, to the end of the age."**

So, "If anyone would come after me, let him deny himself and take up his cross [die, surrender] daily and follow [live, know] me."***

*John 14:23.
**Matthew 28:20.
***Luke 9:23.

4.

The Cross of Abandonment & Communion

The Fourth Word from the Cross

Now from the sixth hour there was darkness over all the land until the ninth hour. And about the ninth hour Jesus cried out with a loud voice, saying, "Eli, Eli, lema sabachthani?" that is, "My God, my God, why have you forsaken me?"

—Matthew 27:45–46

The Forsaken God

My God, my God, why have you forsaken me?
Why are you so far from saving me,
from the words of my groaning?

—Psalm 22:1

The sacredness of these words and the mystery of what happened within the Godhead in the hours of darkness during the crucifixion should give us pause. We are treading on holy ground. The forsaking of the Son and its saving significance can be sensed and experienced more than it can be dissected and explained. George MacDonald attempted to describe the indescribable in his *Unspoken Sermons,*

> The outer darkness is but the most dreadful form of the consuming fire—the fire without light—the darkness visible, the black flame. God hath withdrawn himself, but not lost his hold. His face is turned away, but his hand is laid upon him still. His heart has ceased to beat

into the man's heart, but he keeps him alive by
his fire.*

The mystery of Son riven from the Father, who "made
him to be sin who knew no sin,"** gives us insight into the
very essence of not only sin but also salvation and the
image of God. For to be image bearers of God means, at
its most basic level, that we are created for relationship—
not only with one another but also with a God who is a
community within Himself. The outworking of *sin* is separation and death. Hell is a place where relationship is not.
This leads us to a great mystery: At the cross the Son of
God became something that He was not—*sin*. In light of
this, it is not surprising that some of the first words spoken
in Scripture about humanity were, "It is not good that the
man should be alone."*** And yet this is the very place we
find the Savior of the world. He identifies with us at our
lowest point, our sin. He was isolated and alone, tasting
the hell of total separation. *The Son of sorrows was forsaken* so we could be found and follow. He was abandoned so that we could belong.

*George MacDonald, *Unspoken Sermons* (Whitehorn, Calif.: Johannesen, 1997), 32.

**2 Corinthians 5:21.

***Genesis 2:18.

The Longing to Belong

[1985]

> Loneliness, she said, is when nothing will stick to you,
> when nothing will thrive around you, when you start to
> think that you kill things just by being there.
>
> —Rachel Cusk, *Transit*

We were standing in a swift and frigid mountain river. He turned to me after casting his line and spoke these words: "If you want to be a real man, you have to bite the head off the fish while it's alive!"

I was never going to be his son, but I'm not sure at twelve years old that was a truth I could accept. He had grown up in the same small town as my mom and dad. He was my dad's best friend and my mom's first love. When he was eleven—the age I was when I became his stepson—he was in a serious car crash that killed his father. After this he attempted suicide in the woods with a rifle, which left him with one kidney. As I think back, I believe it is reasonable to assume that the magnitude of this trauma was behind the compression of his interior life that made him emotionally impenetrable most of the time.

He was his mother's pride, a popular and cocky all-star athlete—the very definition of the handsome all-American boy. These factors, combined with my natural disposition toward magical thinking, made my mom's very sudden marriage to this man feel providential. My desire for a dad seemed reasonable, and to be fair, he did try, no matter how inconsistently. The fact is, he was the closest I was ever going to come to having an in-person father, even if he was something more like an emotionally unavailable stunt double for my actual absent father, who would always choose himself over me and my brother. Of course, in true scapegoat fashion, my dad says my mom made the choice for him.*

Here he was teaching me to fish—just me, no one else—and that meant something. I looked back at my stand-in dad with his chiseled jaw, blond hair, yellow-tinted aviators, permanent mustache, and pale skin. Although better looking, he bore more than a passing resemblance to Jeffrey Dahmer, that

---

*Not to state the obvious, but mamas in general are going to consider using alcohol and drugs, with an emphasis on using, as behavior that makes for an unfit environment for their children. To be fair, I'm confident it would not have been worse than living with my two childhood stand-in dads. I do know for sure, based upon the limited time I did spend with my father, that though not at all safe, it would have been more colorful.

infamous murderer who cannibalized young men as a means of exerting power over them.

. . .

This stand-in dad was neither a predator nor a serial killer, so why even mention a name like Dahmer in a book on the cross? I think this deserves reflection. Dahmer's crimes were evil. I would argue they were demonic. But we should remember that after his arrest, all available evidence pointed to his legitimate conversion. I am always surprised and disheartened by the presumption present when people speak about who is saved and who is not. We simply do not know the heart. In regard to fruit for some (like the thief on the cross), a primitive faith placed in Jesus as they are dying is all the fruit there is, so tread carefully. We are not God. It is well documented that Dahmer confessed that his crimes were evil, surrendered to the light of the gospel, repented, was baptized, read his Bible and prayed daily, faithfully attended service, and met with a pastor regularly. He did not shirk justice. He desired it, even demanded it, but Jesus gave him grace.

It is easy to question the authenticity of his conversion due to the nature of his crimes, but I think that has far more to do with our resistance to grace than his sincerity. He was ultimately murdered by a fellow prisoner. In that murderer's mind, and the minds of others, he was not as bad as Dahmer himself. The irony of the scapegoat mechanism is that it is often lost on people. As René Girard so brilliantly declared,

> Almost no one is aware of his own shortcoming. We must question ourselves if we are to understand the enormity of the mystery. Each person must ask what his relationship is to the scapegoat. I am not aware of my own, and I am persuaded that the same holds true for my readers. We only have legitimate enmities. And yet the entire universe swarms with scapegoats.*

Jeffrey Dahmer's violent death makes God's grace and forgiveness no less certain, but it does serve to remind us that we can't escape the fallenness of this world. Our sin, even when forgiven, has the power to inspire sin in others and wreak havoc in our own lives. It is the law of cause and effect. What drives our discomfort with Jesus saving a monster like this is our own refusal to accept that sin is not a measurement of how bad we are but of how good we are not. The saving power of the cross can only offend those who refuse to believe that next to Jesus

---

*René Girard, *The Scapegoat,* trans. Yvonne Freccero (Baltimore: Johns Hopkins University Press, 1986), 41.

we are all monsters, which means that grace is always unfair.

The cross is scandalous—it will always be a place where monsters discover that they are loved and can belong.

. . .

Unfortunately, this comparison to Dahmer works on a couple of levels. It wasn't just that my stand-in dad bore a resemblance to this infamous man, but (metaphorically speaking) he ate me alive emotionally for years with his hot-and-cold "You're like a son to me," "You're not my son" routine. This was soul devouring for me in those formative years. He really did try to love me as much as I tried to make him proud, but the trying on both sides is what became the repellent. What came first, one might wonder, my desperation or his detachment? Ultimately, it didn't matter because that was the mixture we each brought to the table, with increasing volatility over time. The healing the Holy Spirit has brought to me as I work through the complexities of this relationship is what brings grace for the stepdad that could not understand me and the young Josh who longed to be wanted. I would be lying to say it doesn't also bring heartbreak, but Jesus can do more with a broken heart than one hardened by indifference or anger.

The people I have hurt and disappointed the most as a pastor have been the insecure and needy. I say this to my shame, but nothing stifles my ability to love and shuts me down faster than those who are desperate for my approval. Let me say, if you're reading this, and you know me and have experienced that aloofness and irritation from me, I ask for your forgiveness. Know that everyone needs to be known and affirmed, and everyone is insecure from time to time. Our past may be the root for bad behavior, and understanding it the road to real change, but it can never be an excuse.

My struggle, when confronted with someone who is insecure and desperate for my approval, is that it is a mirror held up, exposing what was at play for much of the twenty-seven years leading up to my own conversion. Insecurity can still get me today. My sense of invisibility and my cringeworthy desperation to be loved and appreciated guaranteed I would not receive what I was seeking for so much of my life. This makes it unbearable when I see it in others, and I truly say that with a heavy heart.

. . .

There we were. The river rushed. The challenge had been made, and I wanted it more than anything. The sad desperation in me to belong and to be seen was so overwhelming that at the time, I couldn't see that becoming a man by biting a head off a living fish was not actually a thing, and even if it was, it was not normal. I try not to overthink why he said it at all or, worse, why I did what follows.

Within minutes of the statement being released into the ether, I hooked a beautiful twelve-to-fourteen-inch rainbow trout. It was as if the universe was for once on my side. My will had become bound to the absurdity of his words. The sacrifice had been provided, and there could be no divine or mortal intervention. I called out. He turned. I pulled that fish off the hook—rod held between my knees, river rushing around my feet, the offering wriggling and gasping in my determined death grip—and momentarily lifted it to the heavens. I remember its iridescent skin, how it shimmered in the sun as it fought to be free. But its freedom was not possible when mine hung in the balance. So before it could slip from my hands or I could question the decision, I placed its head in my mouth and bit down.

I could feel its mouth open within mine as my teeth severed its spine. My stomach churned as I was quickly overcome by the taste of iron from biting into its heart, which rested at the base of its throat. I used my hand to tear the body free and quickly spit the head into the moving river in a primal triumph that had overridden the queasiness. He laughed so hard he fell down in the river.*

---

*My stepdad provided for the family. He took the time to teach me to work with my hands, to saddle and ride a horse, to catch and throw a baseball, to wrestle and play pool, and to catch and clean a fish, but most of the time he

In thirty seconds something had changed, but I wasn't a man. As I stared down at what remained of the twitching fish—alien out of water, incomplete without a head, dead but still fighting to live, soon to be consumed—I understood that this was a change in the wrong direction. My ache to belong only grew.

---

was indifferent to my presence. He laughed with me, but he could be cruel, also laughing at me for my sensitivity or tickling me in front of my friends until I wet my pants, which left me so utterly humiliated that only my inner rage could hold the tears back.

He bought me my first guitar and taught me how to play "Song for Adam" by Jackson Browne. He purchased my first car and taught me how to drive a stick shift with reasonable patience; I ground the gears of his little Volkswagen pickup in the high school parking lot.

And yet his fuse grew increasingly short over time. He challenged me to fight more than once and ultimately kicked me out of the house when I was seventeen. Why? I spilled a bucket of oil on the garage floor and tried to clean it up with water, which made an even greater mess. This incident was the catalyst for my mom bringing an end to her third marriage and my dad of seven years.

This man was the same man who took me out to lunch after their separation, telling me through tears that he was so sorry, how much he loved me, that I would always be a son to him, and then never talked to me again. Yet as I write this thirty years later to the month, I find myself grateful for him, even missing him.

It's Not Good
to Be Alone

We're all on each other's food chain. All of us. It's an individual
sport. Welcome to the meaning of *individual*. We're each deeply
alone here. It's what we all have in common, this aloneness.

—**David Foster Wallace**, *Infinite Jest*

It is nearly impossible to understand why Jesus was
forsaken, or what He was correcting, if we do not
understand what went wrong. Loneliness today is so
commonplace that we may be reaching a point in history where we can no longer see that the isolation
of our solipsistic* age is one of the central reasons
we hurt. I must ask, "When have we ever been best
alone?" To even scratch the surface of the forsaking of

---

*Solipsistic means self-centered, but it communicates more than being selfish. It is a
philosophical structure that has permeated the secular age with the belief that the
individual is the ground of being, not God. French existentialist philosopher Jean-
Paul Sartre summed it up perfectly in his slim volume *Existentialism Is a Humanism*,
first published in 1946. He wrote, "Since God does not exist and we all must die,
everything is permissible. One experience is as good as another, so what matters is
simply to acquire as many of them as possible." Jean-Paul Sartre, *Existentialism Is a
Humanism* (New Haven, Conn.: Yale University, 2007), 78.

God, we must ask what Scripture says about life together.

Right now, I am trying to finish writing this book—
which I'd describe as trying to find my way through a
labyrinth blind while simultaneously performing a root
canal on my soul—in a cabin, alone, on the Deschutes
River. It is a stunning setting. The ancient cliffs jut up behind the rushing waters that fork in front of the cabin. It is
a fly fisherman's paradise and a bird-watcher's daydream,
with rainbow trout surfacing below and osprey circling
above. Yet, three days in, the external beauty has only
become a constant reminder of the lack of beauty found
in my brain and how much more I would love this place
if Darcy and the kids were here with me.

There is a mystery that should be unpacked with care
in the proclamation God spoke over Adam—whose very
name means *humankind*—before the fall amid a creation
that was good. God declared, "It is not good for the man
to be alone."*

This is a profound statement. It goes beyond the marriage union and puts a nail in the coffin of our romance
with hyperindividualism. Here in the garden we have
sinless, God-breathed man with God, and God says
that man alone—that is, without other humans—is incomplete even with God. I am immediately reminded
of a popular, pithy maxim attributed to Augustine, "He
who has God has everything; he who has everything

*Genesis 2:18, NIV.

but God has nothing."* The second half of the statement is true, but the first half is problematic on multiple levels, and, I believe, this sentiment has fed the temptation throughout church history to turn faith into a private affair. It may be fair to say the one who has God alone has the One who is the source of everything, but according to God, that same one does not have everything he needs.

It is not that God was saying to Adam, "I am not enough," but that He created him for others like himself. It was in Adam and Eve's relationship together, before the fall, that the image of God was most fully realized. I do not believe it is speculative to declare that in their togetherness, before sin entered their story, they were best suited to commune with God. Together they brought forth the divine proclamation, it is "very good."** Maybe this is the reason for the gap between the creation of Adam and Eve—to make Adam feel his incompleteness. For unlike God, who is triune and whose oneness flows out of the perfect communion of love between the Father, Son, and Spirit, man is not and never has been a community within himself. And since the fall, humanity in its endless search for meaning apart from God has become a menagerie of artificial needs.

---

*I have personally found no evidence that this quote was ever spoken or written by Augustine. However I have both heard in sermons and read in books this general sentiment too many times to count.

**Genesis 1:31.

. . .

In Genesis 1, we are given a compressed account of the creation story. On the sixth day God uniquely created man and woman in His own image:

> So God created mankind in his own image,
>   in the image of God he created them;
>   male and female he created them.*

They "image" God together and were blessed as co-laborers with God over His creation. God saw what He had made and said it was "very good."

Genesis 2 is not a second creation story (as some critics have theorized), but a more detailed account of the sixth day of the creation narrative. It is here we find the gap between the creation of man from the dirt and the creation of woman from the man. Though different, both equally carry the breath of God in them—so let us not in any way view this as a diminishment of women. Besides, all humanity since has carried both realities, for we come from the flesh and return to the dirt.

It is here we find man alone with God but without a suitable companion, to which God declared, "It is *not good.*"** For God, in the creation of Eve, gave Adam someone fitted to commune with him, a companion who was

*Genesis 1:27.

**Genesis 2:18, emphasis added.

different, who was like him, who was human. And it was in their sameness and uniqueness that the two together became one, and it was "very good."*

How strange that the "very good" union becomes the catalyst for a very "not good" situation. The fall ruptured relationships, not only between Adam and Eve but with God as well. By the close of Genesis 3, sin has entered the story, guilt and shame have taken hold, humanity has been alienated and exiled, death is reigning, the serpent is ruling, and the earth is groaning.

. . .

God then declared a mysterious word over our first parents in their fallen state that found its solution in Jesus: "Behold, the man has become like one of us in knowing good and evil."** This is not a positive statement. To paraphrase, the triune God was declaring, "Behold, humanity has become what I did not intend. They have become their own gods."

We can think it is cruel that our first parents were banished from the garden to work the ground that was cursed, but we must remember that the ground was cursed for their sake. Why? Because humanity in a fallen state, left in paradise, would never see the need for God. Modern history has proven this, for as our prosperity increases,

*Genesis 1:31.
**Genesis 3:22.

our pleasures multiply, and our mortality is extended, godlessness and despair increase as well. None of these things can save us from sin or that fearful owl of death. The ground was cursed because it is in the toil and, if I may borrow from the language of recovery groups, our bottoming out that we find our need. We will never be prepared for life after death if we do not taste death in life.

. . .

When we look at this tragic event through the lens of the *incarnation,* we find another insight into its mystery. As it says in the first chapter of the gospel of John, "The Word became flesh and made his dwelling among us. We have seen his glory, the glory of the one and only Son, who came from the Father, full of grace and truth."*

God with us and for us. He stepped into the mess of our first parents and made it His own, and here the story takes on even greater meaning. For there never has been a time before the fall or after that it was good for man to be alone. The creation of the two, along with the fall they produced, was never the end but the means to the end. For God gave the great corrective through the woman's seed. True completeness was made possible.

The eternal Son was fitted into the likeness of sinful flesh. Jesus, the God-man, identified not just with our humanity but also with our lowest point—our sin. He

*John 1:14, NIV.

walked directly into the dysfunction, incompleteness, and alienation brought forth by our first parents. When Jesus was about to be crucified, Pilate proclaimed the same thing God declared over humanity in the garden after the fall. Scripture says, "So Jesus came out, wearing the crown of thorns and the purple robe. Pilate said to them, 'Behold the man!'"*

Pilate did not see that his sarcastic statement was the truest thing he had ever said. Jesus is man as God intended man to be; He is the representative man, the one for the many and the many in the one. On the cross we find Jesus, the judge and the judged, in our place. It is here that God wove the liability that led to the fall into His redemptive history in the once-and-for-all sacrifice of Jesus. In being forsaken for us all, He made our reconciliation a reality and a future fall an impossibility. It is hard not to see in this mystery the logic of the famous proclamation, "O Felix Culpa!"**

All that to say, if God thought the risk of putting humans together was better than the incompleteness of man alone, we should as well.

This is why loving God and one another are inextricably linked. For Jesus, in the loneliness of the cross, tore down every wall of separation. When asked what was most important, He answered, "'Love the Lord your God with all your heart and with all your soul and with

*John 19:5.

**"O Happy Fault!"

all your mind.' This is the first and greatest commandment. And the second is like it: 'Love your neighbor as yourself.' All the Law and the Prophets hang on these two commandments."*

He was forsaken so we could be together.

*Matthew 22:37–40, NIV.

I've Got You

[2014]

> But suppose we fly from the One, what will our flight
> profit us, if it is love from which we are escaping?
> The assault of God embraces the whole man.

—Karl Barth, *The Epistle to the Romans*

I could barely understand her as she hysterically
said, "Joshua, your dad has been flown to Anchorage. He has had a heart attack and has a ruptured
esophagus from a bender. The doctor said he is currently in an induced coma, and there is a strong
chance he will not make it."

My aunt, who is my dad's only sibling, was so
distraught, I realized I had to go as much for her
as for me. It was a cold, rainy Saturday morning. I
told her I would fly out that day and hung up the
phone.

Within four hours I was staring out a window
watching the rain form small streams that moved
horizontally along the glass. I was in the back row

on a flight to Anchorage. The seat would not recline, nor would my heart.

I was nervous and afraid of what I would find lying in that hospital bed. Besides when I flew my dad down for a couple of weeks two years earlier, up to this point my witness and love had only been in word. I had an overwhelming sensation that I should show up and not speak the gospel but embody it, love him as his son, be with him in his loneliness, care for him in his sickness, and be patient in his fear and anger. This is not me encouraging silence, for doing good for someone does not, in and of itself, lead one to Christ. God has chosen to draw others to Himself through the witness of His people, which means we must introduce Him with words backed by acts of love. My dad had heard the words—he needed to know I loved him regardless of what he chose to believe.

By the time I landed, Dad had already been brought out of the induced coma and was waiting in confusion for my arrival. He didn't truly believe I was coming.

I walked into that sterile ICU room overwhelmed by his presence and the smell. He looked dead—his skin was gray, and his eyes were jaundice yellow from alcohol poisoning and bleeding out. His face and legs were swollen so tight from edema that they looked like they could split open. Covered in tubes and breathing irregularly, he looked at me as if he had seen a ghost. There was confusion, fear, and embarrassment in his cloudy eyes. We stared silently as I tried to adjust to the shock. After what felt like an eternity, I was able to get out a shaky "Hey, Dad."

"Hello, son. You look good."

His voice was a rough whisper, and I noticed tears in his eyes. While trying to hold back tears, I responded gently with a smirk, "You look horrible! What did you do?"

"Now don't you start with me, Joshua. Your old man isn't dead yet, and I can still kick your butt!"

"I am positive there is a zero percent chance of that happening, although you might kill me with your stench!"

"Oh, f— you."

We both started laughing.

"I've missed you, Dad."

"You too, son."

He got quiet and looked out the window. I stepped into that stifling space, sat next to him, and gently took his hand. He gripped it as if his life depended upon it, but he had little strength. Death had come near—his body was ravaged by it, but he had somehow escaped.

He had gotten into a fight with his old lady and went on a drinking binge, downing three-fifths of a bottle of Crown Royal* in a day before passing out. She found him in a pool of blood from the rupture.

---

*A Canadian whiskey that comes in a purple cloth sack, which I guess is meant to make overdrinking somehow regal.

Although she was drunk as well, she had enough gumption to call 911—another hour and he would not have made it.

My dad has had hepatitis C since the nineties and had already had three strokes, COPD, prostate cancer, cirrhosis, and a plethora of other things. Two days before writing this fragment we talked, and he said he still smokes two to three packs of Camel Red cigarettes and drinks more than a fifth of a bottle of vodka a day. We joked that he is like a cockroach that cannot be killed. The number of times he has been at death's door are too many to count. This event was over seven years ago, and not much has changed when it comes to his nonexistent self-care.

After a short time, I went out to the nursing station of the ICU and asked if someone could give my dad a shower. You can smell the dysfunction of internal organs when someone drinks that heavily. He also had not bathed, I'm sure, in weeks. I was staying in the room with him and told the nurses that would not be possible until he had been cleaned. They were kind and extremely accommodating, promising to send someone right in. I entered back into that suffocating space and told Dad that I was having a nurse come and give him a shower. He became extremely agitated and started swearing at me, to which I responded, "Listen, Dad. You have two choices—either the nurse showers you or I do."

He realized his agitation was leading to difficulty

breathing, that I was dead serious, and that the nurse (who was a kind and attractive young woman) was a much more appealing option than me, so he conceded.

As my father lay there, he told me he needed to use the bathroom but had not been able to walk yet. The nurse said I could help him get to the toilet, which was complicated because he was hooked up to an IV. I slowly helped him get to his feet. He was so weak, and his equilibrium was all off. Even so, he still put up a fight, telling me he didn't need help.

I got frustrated and released him. As he walked slowly toward the bathroom, holding on to the roller that the IV bag hung from, his hospital gown fully open, exposing his naked backside, suddenly he paused and began to sway like an old tree uprooted. Just as he was about to fall, I caught him from behind—his gown open and dirty body against mine. Embarrassed, he began to fight me, cursing, demanding I let go. But I gripped him in my arms and spoke to him like a child: "Dad, it's okay. I've got you. Relax, I've got you."

I felt his body relax against mine, and in that moment my rigid heart melted as my father allowed me to love him. He needed my embrace, and I needed to embrace him. It is a strange thing to embody a theological truth; it was in that moment that I began to understand the power of grace. Many have been surprised at my willingness to engage with a man who was never there for me, who is still a stranger in many ways. But he is my father, and I am his son.

Besides, how can I forget Jesus embraced me and held me close even when I, at twenty-seven, was fighting Him tooth and nail?

✝

Make Haste Slowly

I have met with but one or two persons in the course of my life
who understood the art of Walking, that is, of taking walks—
who had a genius, so to speak, for *sauntering*.

—Henry David Thoreau, "Walking"

The restless, distracted energy of our technological age
has risen to a fever pitch. With each advancement, we are
bound closer together into a collective fragmentation
without intimacy. The loneliness and relational divides
that flow back to the beginning of recorded history are
being amplified rather than silenced. We engage in everything from religious practices, mindfulness, yoga, and
exercise to television, sex, food, drink, and drugs. We do
all this to escape. As Don DeLillo wrote in his brilliant
and funny novel *White Noise*, "That's why people take
vacations. Not to relax or find excitement or see new
places. To escape the death that exists in routine things."*

The forsaken God has entered into and dealt with this

*Don DeLillo, *White Noise*, 25th anniversary ed. (New York: Penguin, 2009), 248.

cosmic loneliness, yet often followers of the crucified King are just as lonely as the rest. What is missing?

There is a classical adage that might prove helpful: *Festina lente,* which means "to make haste slowly." A crab and butterfly first symbolized this saying. Its meaning lies in the paradox that existence is not meant to be static or careless but defined by conscientious and careful movement.

As one who leans into life with a relatively free-spirited disposition, when I look at the crab-and-butterfly image, I find myself uneasy at the way the butterfly seems held back by the crab's clamp upon her wings. But it is that tendency that has led me to make many grievous errors throughout my forty-eight years of life. The crab is a necessary reminder that our movement must be anchored in thoughtfulness.

Walking is a beautiful metaphor used throughout Scripture to symbolize both movement and intimacy. This is a lovely reminder that the goal of the Christian life is not arriving at a destination but knowing God. This is the very heart of what it means to be a disciple.

Walking can be sustained for much greater distances than running because it is motion essentially without strife. It is progress that is truly conscientious of its surroundings. Our walk is not a lonely journey, isolated in pursuit of self-actualization. For Christians, our place in this world is discovered in walking with God toward others. We are free in Christ, but we are not free from Him or one another. We cannot embody the individualistic worldview that says, "I am best when I'm alone." Sadly, it is often Christian leaders who follow this path. Solitude must never be separation. We cannot and must not escape the world or the people in it. That is a false holiness that drains the forsaking of Jesus of all meaning. It fights against the very One who tore down the walls of separation by building new ones.

. . .

I take such comfort that the first time we find the word *walk* in the Scriptures, it is used to describe God Himself walking through the garden in search of our first parents: "They heard the sound of the LORD God walking in the garden in the cool of the day, and the man and his wife hid themselves from the presence of the LORD God among the trees of the garden."* He wasn't walking to clear His mind but to share His heart. While God was walking, the center of His creation, *humanity,* was hiding. You see, this is the movement of a God seeking what is lost. It is grace that is both restorative and relational in nature.**

---

*Genesis 3:8.

**When I think about the walks I have taken with my wife, in order for the company to be sweet and the conversation rich, our strides have to match. Trying to hold Darcy's hand when our rhythm is out of sync is not only difficult but also distracting. Worse still are those distracted moments when I have walked in front of Darcy, unaware of how I have left her trailing behind, or in my laziness, I refused to walk with her at all.

Isn't this how we often treat our God? God loves us, pursues us, saves us, and calls us to follow Him—that is, to walk with Him and know Him by the power of His Spirit within us. Yet how often do we refuse His company and His leading, or blaze our own trail, thinking He should follow us?

When our first parents stopped walking and started hiding, they lost so much more than just the garden. They lost God, each other, and themselves. But the hope that we are given in Scripture is that God has always been moving toward us in mercy and has fully walked toward us in Jesus, who was forsaken so that we could be found. He has restored communion and is ever calling us back to Himself.

Jesus, the *forsaken God,* calls us to walk with Him and walk in Him into the world He died for, the world He is reconciling to Himself. For He is the firstborn over a new humanity, and to walk in Him is to walk in newness of life.

. . .

The normative movement of Jesus is not away from the world of people, and all the problems that come with it, but into the midst of its pain. He has always been a God who pursues and meets people in their sin. This means we don't need solitude to find Him, as helpful as it may be from time to time. His Spirit is not interested in keeping us in the comfort of the upper room. We cannot forget the Holy Spirit is first and foremost a missionary Spirit whose chief role is to point the world to Jesus and declare that the world has not been abandoned. Walking with Jesus is being led by the Spirit into places of such brokenness that if we were left to our own devices, like our first parents, we would rather hide.

And let's be honest. We often do.

As we walk with Jesus, who is our beginning, our end, and our way through the in-between, let us be careful to think of our progress not as a hero's journey but as relational, intimate, and (due to our mixture) often clumsy. In other words, to walk with God is defined by progress that is most clearly seen by others and is often barely perceptible to ourselves.

If you are like me, you may find yourself thinking, "I am not good company, and what can I possibly have to offer Jesus?" The answer, my friend, is simple: *Yourself.* Christ doesn't choose to use sinners because they're strong, wise, or gifted—strength is a positive impediment—but because He's gracious, and He seems to enjoy using the weak things of this world to confound, and even reach, the wise.

. . .

The butterfly has been used in the history of the church to symbolize resurrection, metamorphosis, and transformation by the Spirit's activity in our lives. But what of the crab? While there is no use of the crab as a symbol that I can find in church history, I will say this: As the crab in the original *festina lente* emblem symbolized a grounding or foundation for healthy movement, so the cross of Christ must be the center and grounding of our lives.

If Jesus is the way,* and there is only one way to go, then there are a thousand ways to lose the way, fall from

*See John 14:6.

it, or even run from it—see Abraham, Elijah, Jonah, and Peter. We will lose the way, but that is why Jesus came, why it is good news that the gospel is down-to-earth, and why it's not good to travel alone.

The cross is our center, our equilibrium, and our compass. It is a constant reminder that if you've dug yourself into a hole, His love goes deeper still; if you've lost your way, He will leave the others to find you again and again; if you have fallen, that's the whole reason He came; and if you have run away, the cross can lead you home. Jesus was forsaken so that you could be found. He is with you, so arise and return to your Father. He loves you and longs to embrace you. We belong, and the cross and our forsaken King are the proof. So *festina lente*. Let us make haste.

Slowly.

5.

The Cross of Suffering & Satisfaction

The Fifth Word from the Cross

After this, Jesus, knowing that all was now finished,
said (to fulfill the Scripture), "I thirst."

—John 19:28

I say to you—and I beg you to believe me—multiply these tiny
triumphs by a million, add them all together, and they are
nothing—less than nothing, a positive impediment—measured
against one draught of that living water Christ offers to the
spiritually thirsty, irrespective of who or what they are.

—Malcolm Muggeridge, *Jesus Rediscovered*

The Thirsty River

> Jesus answered her, "If you knew the gift of God, and
> who it is that is saying to you, 'Give me a drink,' you would
> have asked him, and he would have given you living water. . . .
> Whoever drinks of the water that I will give him will never
> be thirsty again. The water that I will give him will become in
> him a spring of water welling up to eternal life."
>
> **—John 4:10, 14**

The fifth word from the cross is the most succinct. It is the cry of anguish that holds the suffering of the world in it. It is the terrible beauty and mystery of Jesus the God-*man* at the physical and spiritual boundary of pain. Jesus has drunk the cup of suffering to its final dregs, and He is left thirsty. In becoming *sin* He has tasted and conquered our enemies. Here the forsaken God is so fully identified with the frailty of our fallen humanity that we can hear that *fearful owl* death itself in His cry.

Like a runner about to collapse on the finish line, He has journeyed through the outer darkness of *sin* and its separating power without collapsing under its weight or surrendering to its call. We may never understand suffering, but we can trust Jesus understands our frailty and *sin* better than we even can. Why? How could He understand sin if He never sinned?

He understands because He took sin into Himself with a death grip—all of it without causing any of it.*

He who knew no sin became *sin*. His thirst is the physical suffering of His humanity dying and the spiritual suffering—that mystery within the Godhead hidden from view—He endured as the eternal Son, separated from the Father and the Spirit. The forsaken King holds sin in as He moves toward His final play—the River of Life has seemingly run dry, "for the wages of sin is death."** And there it is, Nietzsche was right, *we have killed God*.*** His blood is on our hands, and we are guilty—all of us! We need not despair—His blood spilled is how we taste Life itself.**** It is the greatest sleight of hand in cosmic history. For the cross is the place where God played the game by the Enemy's rules and commandeered Satan's weapon, death itself, as the vehicle by which He, the God-man,

---

*In the parable of the strong man in Luke 11:21–22, Jesus says, "When a strong man, fully armed, guards his own palace, his goods are safe; but when one stronger than he attacks him and overcomes him, he takes away his armor in which he trusted and divides his spoil." It is my belief that Jesus is pointing to the cross. Satan is the *strong man* and Jesus is the *stronger man* who removes his weapons (sin, darkness, and death), setting the captives free. This is accomplished through the incarnation, which includes Jesus's life, death, resurrection, and ascension and the sending of His Spirit.

**Romans 6:23.

***"The madman sprang into their midst and pierced them with his glances. 'Where has God gone?' he cried. 'I shall tell you. *We have killed him*—you and I.'" Friedrich Nietzsche, *Thus Spoke Zarathustra*, trans. R. J. Hollingdale (London: Penguin, 1974), 125.

****"And the blood of Jesus his Son cleanses us from all sin" (1 John 1:7).

would carry sin and death into the grave. He reversed the curse once and for all "by becoming a curse for us."*

The kingdom of darkness thought it was victorious as the Son of God cried out, as He tasted the anguish of separation. Jesus was like the rich man in His own parable who, in torment, begged Abraham to send the beggar Lazarus, whom he had mistreated in life, to dip the end of his finger in the water to cool his tongue, to experience even a few seconds of respite from his eternal anguish.**

But victory belonged to the Thirsty River Himself who went through the physical and spiritual thirst for the joy that was set before Him: You! He is thirsty for you. Do you thirst for Him? This is the door to our satisfaction and the place where pity dies and gratitude, in spite of and often through our pain, is birthed.

*Galatians 3:13.

**See Luke 16:24.

The Horse

[1985]

Faith has been broken, tears must be cried
Let's do some living after we die

—The Rolling Stones, "Wild Horses"

I was more than a little excited the summer I discovered that my second stand-in dad had a horse, and he was willing to teach me to ride. Our mobile home sat at the foot of what are appropriately called the Horse Heaven Hills. Over my first summer in that desert wilderness of the Columbia Basin, I would feed, brush, and saddle up our beautiful, feisty, half-Arabian, half-quarter horse, Silver, every day. I rode up and down the dusty trails of the hills for hours in the dry heat.

My competence and confidence grew in correspondence to the muscles in my inner thighs, but the bond that grew with the horse—in a place where I had not yet made any friends—was most powerful. When school started, he would walk parallel to me each morning as I traveled down our gravel road. He would neigh and throw his large head back in frustration as he came to the end of his pen.

I always felt guilty leaving him behind, but nothing compared to the shame I felt on the day he was sold, which happened because I wasn't riding him any longer. My equestrian season had come to an abrupt close on the day I became afraid of the horse I loved. Like riding a motorcycle, if riding a horse is done with any regularity, an accident is unavoidable.

Now, riding a horse is as exhilarating as it is terrifying. When riding, you are on the back of an extremely large living, intelligent thing, whose average top speed is thirty to thirty-five miles per hour and who weighs between 900 and 1,100 pounds. Horses that are not regularly ridden and don't have rapport with a rider can be mean. They can sneak up behind you and bite you (which really hurts), rub you against fencing, trees, or whatever is available to get you off them, buck you off, or in the worst case kick you or trample you to death. Besides biting me, Silver did none of these things. He wasn't responsible for my fear, but like the boys who bullied me, he could sense it and didn't like the smell.

Here is what happened in the spring of '85.

—Riding bareback down a gravel road with my

girlfriend, Nicky—whom I never kissed but who once punched me in the stomach and made me cry—on a retired racehorse named April.

—April running top speed and refusing to stop.

—Nicky and I in a panic, pulling so hard on the reins that her nose was facing us.

—Coming to the end of the road and taking what felt like a ninety-degree turn at forty miles per hour.

—Nicky and I flying off the horse, which was my fault—she would not have fallen had she been riding solo.

—Her flying into a ball like the experienced rider she was, receiving only minor bruises, and me in an upside-down-Christ pose, landing on the back of my head.

—Being covered in blood while Nicky is screaming, "You're losing too much blood. You're going to die!"

—Woozy, covered in blood and sobbing while hugging Nicky with the seriousness of a romantic last rite, covering her in blood.

—Realizing that at eleven, I wasn't ready to die and waving down a truck looking like an attempted murder victim.

—A kind cowboy with a calm face and (in my memory) the voice of Sam Elliott saying in a strangely inoffensive and soothing way, "Try not to get blood on my seat, son."

I was rushed to the hospital, had the back of my

head shaved, received four stitches for what was only a half-inch cut, and was sent home with a raging headache and nausea from the concussion. This event created a serious fear of horses that persists to this day and a concise close to my year on horseback, not to mention the end of a friendship. Sorry, buddy!

. . .

I didn't want to be a cowboy. My refusal to "get back in the saddle," as they say, guaranteed it. Only an unquenchable thirst that flows from an unshakable love can overcome the fear that follows a traumatic event. At eleven, I never understood the risk of riding. My faith in my ability to ride was based not on experience but on the fearlessness that can flow from youthful ignorance. A faith that works flows from the right affections. How we come through the crisis of failure and the doubt that follows reveals the depth of our love or the lack thereof. This is why failure has the power to fortify our faith or cause us to abandon it.

There is an old cowboy saying: "There ain't a horse that can't be rode. There ain't a cowboy that can't be throwed."

Well, it may be true in terms of riding horses—I wasn't cut out to be a real cowboy, and my fear got the best of me. However, if I was to apply this same concept to ministry in a place like Portland, which truly is the Wild West, I might just be a real cowboy. Failure in ministry is like falling off the horse; I'm not sure if I am courageous or stupid, but I have gotten back in the saddle more times than I can count. I've faced criticisms, mental breakdowns, sleepless nights, demonic attacks, shingles, and complete adrenal crash. I've sought distractions, attempted various escapes, shown destructive behavior, and chose the influence of drink to ease the stress rather than the Spirit.

As I write this, I can say no matter how much I hurt, how unhealthy I can be—even at times unhappy—I just can't seem to get away, nor do I want to, from the One who met me twenty-three years ago and told me I was loved, who showed me trying and climbing was not the answer but dying and rising with Him was. I love Him too much to keep Him to myself; I simply cannot. Sometimes I'm a bull in a china shop, my zeal exceeds my gifts, and I fall. Sometimes I'm still the boy under the bed paralyzed by fear, and I fall. Sometimes I get unhealthy and simply don't have the strength, and I fall. But every time I'm tempted to stay down, I am reminded of the exhilaration of following Him who is the way, the truth, and the life.

A real cowboy, like a real Christian, is not defined by any particular giftedness—it's just who he is. He will likely have a gun, but he might be a terrible shot. He will always be identifiable by the boots, the hat, the buckle, and the denim, but he might have terrible style. He will always have a horse, but he may not be a great rider. But one thing he will always do: Get back in the saddle.

A Cluster of Needs

You made us for yourself and our hearts find
no peace until they rest in you.

—Saint Augustine, *Confessions*

Everyone hurts, and most of us have experienced those moments where a heartbreak becomes so significant that we wish everything could just go quiet for a moment. However, most people know innately that no matter how bad we hurt, suffering is still living, and as long as we are living, tomorrow might be better. This is why we are drawn to stories of survival against impossible odds. We agree with Tolstoy, "If you are alive—live."*

With the demise of community in the twentieth century, the exaltation of the individual, the rejection of dogma in every institution, and the supremacy of the personal narrative as the ground of being, I'm afraid Huxley's "brave new world" isn't coming, it's here. We are gifted at

---

*Leo Tolstoy, *War and Peace,* trans. Louise and Aylmer Maude, vol. 1, illustrated and rev. ed. (London: Collector's Library, 2004), 426.

being critical but are unable to critically think through the reasons that make us so. There is a terrifying willingness to turn away from thousands of years of world history without even considering, for a moment, that every generation is the outcome of what has come before.

We may forget our history, but the powerful ideas that have accumulated over time and shape this current moment we live in don't stop because of our ignorance of them. We only impede our own ability to understand the philosophical constructs that undergird the things we believe, not only about the world but also about ourselves. I can deny the existence of the wall behind me as much as I want, but I cannot stop the wall from being there. Its reality doesn't cease because of my refusal to acknowledge it. Disbelief cannot make the wall cease; it only hinders my understanding of what holds the house up.*

Our desire to curate our own bespoke spirituality comes from our need to worship, and the influencers of social media are the priests and priestesses of the moment. They are there as the cheerleaders of the "god" within you, to defend, popularize, and promote endless and new variations of that mystery religion of old—the woman who rides the beast, Babylon. This is Religion

---

*The Spirit cannot bring to remembrance what we have not taken the time to learn. How can we apply the truth of Jesus to the lies of a world under the sway of the devil if we do not even know there are philosophical constructs creating our world of illusion? There is a cognitive principle that we must understand: All we know is all there is. Remember, our ignorance is not innocence. That is terrifying in an age where our kids will turn to TikTok and Instagram for news, beauty, and advice, Snapchat for conversation, and shows like *Euphoria*—with its mesmerizing and graphic nihilism—for inspiration.

with a capital R, and its adherents can never satisfy its demand for blood. Its followers are asked to climb to nothing and ultimately jump from nothing; the ladder is so tall that only a few make it to the top, and yet so many get on it. How can the collective deception, "You can do and be whatever you want to be," lead us anywhere other than despair?

The spiritual thirst that worship of self produces is as unquenchable as it is deadly. But the illusions we drink in are like the vinegar that was given to Jesus. Our misguided quest for satisfaction explains the collective grief and emotional dissonance we feel when our celebrities take their own lives. It is not driven by our concern for the one who has died. It is about us; we have lived our fantasies vicariously through them.

The desire to be known and loved is at the core of what it means to be divine image bearers. But the strange allure of fame, that rare unicorn that often turns out to be a manticore,* is the lust of the eyes, the lust of the flesh, and the pride of life.**

When a celebrity dies, our idolatry is exposed, and its ugliness is revealed. By committing suicide, the celebrity

*Manticore is a mythical creature that devours its victims whole with three rows of razor-sharp teeth.

**Fame is not defined by wealth—there are thousands of billionaires and not many are known—but real fame cannot be sustained without wealth, for wealth is the diet of fame. It represents (for us mere mortals in our material world) fulfillment and immortality, and, among young people today, its illusion goes so deep that being a famous influencer has become—as ludicrous as it sounds—the leading career goal among American high school students. See the introduction in David Brooks's *The Road to Character* (New York: Random House, 2015).

rejects what we believe would make us complete. When those who have made it to the top of human achievement jump down to their deaths, they communicate to the rest of us below, still struggling to get to base camp, "Sorry, but there is nothing up here."

For those who lack the emotional or mental fortitude to begin the journey toward self-discovery, as well as those who have climbed without satisfaction to the top but lack the will to jump, there remains the collective genius of fallen minds in this technological age. These minds, by some Faustian deal, have provided us with unceasing variation—systems of illusion to help dull, even silence, the nagging voice of conscience. From addiction to entertainment, from sex to religion, our modes of escape seem to be without number, propagating the great deception that life can somehow be lived without living.

What we do not seem to understand is that the illusions are so complex, so integrated into our daily lives, and so universally accepted that we are often blind to what is being communicated with such seductive force. It is a partial truth followed by a satanic lie. Life may be impossible, and without question it is terminal, but it is false to think the best we can do is escape it.

Whatever we are looking for is not up there; neither is it down here in our empty attempts to find respite through satisfying our artificial needs. That being said, I do promise the longing at the center of the heartbreaks we endure has a corresponding satisfaction, or we wouldn't long for it. Its permanent satisfaction will not be found in me or the world around me. Our answer rests in the crucified and resurrected King who understands our thirst and is Himself our satisfaction.

He is the *one stronger* who has set us free from *the strong man*, Satan himself. The Enemy's weapons were pillaged through the death of Jesus, who has come to set the captives free.* "But now in Christ Jesus you who once were far away have been brought near by the blood of Christ."**

The immovability of these words reveals the terrible beauty and inexorable love of the crucified King. His cross is the vital center and the key to entering the mess of existence because there we find God Himself getting into the mess and making it His own. As P. T. Forsyth, the great Scottish theologian, wrote, "You do not understand Christ till you understand His cross."***

*Luke 11:21–22, see earlier footnote on page 134 (in the Thirsty River section) about this passage.

**Ephesians 2:13, NIV.

***P. T. Forsyth, *The Cruciality of the Cross* (Eugene, Ore.: Wipf and Stock, 1997), 26.

Freedom Is Fragile

The life of a follower of Jesus could be summed up
in three words: adjusting to freedom.

—Chad Bird, *Upside-Down Spirituality*

As a deer pants for flowing streams,
so pants my soul for you, O God.
My soul thirsts for God,
for the living God.

—Psalm 42:1–2

Freedom is fragile. The moment the Son sets us free—
which, biblically speaking, only truly happens for the re-
generate—we now have the possibility, like children
learning to walk, to fall on our faces. As Paul emphati-
cally declared to the church of Galatia, "You, my brothers
and sisters, were called to be free. But do not use your
freedom to indulge the flesh; rather, serve one another
humbly in love."*

*Galatians 5:13, NIV.

He wouldn't have made a statement like that unless misuse of freedom was a real danger. As a friend and mentor of mine said when Door of Hope began, "It may be God's church, but don't think for a second you can't blow it up!"

Falling from grace is not losing what we have received, but we can and will, more than we want to admit because of the law of mixture, misuse our freedom, temporarily losing our way and our sense of what it means to be forgiven and accepted. This is not a denial of sanctification or a cheapening of grace—God clearly keeps what is His—but we would exceed the boundaries of Scripture and deny human history if we claim it is not possible to make a mess of the freedom Jesus gives. We need not argue over the mechanics of this.* One cannot read the Scripture without seeing this tension. There must be a response of repentance and trust on our side, and that cannot happen without an intervention and drawing on God's side. God may always be "previous," but we must surrender to His revelation.

Nothing has comforted me more in my own messy life than His words to Peter and the disciples in the upper room: "Will you really lay down your life for me? Very truly I tell you, before the rooster crows, you will disown

---

*Rationalistic attempts to penetrate the mystery of divine sovereignty and human responsibility have led to many monstrous speculations around the nature and character of God. It is always a dangerous game to play psychoanalyst with God. He doesn't need a shrink but surrender.

me three times! Do not let your hearts be troubled. You believe in God; believe also in me."*

If I could rephrase, Jesus was saying, "Listen, Peter, you are going to turn your back on me, and the rest of you will leave me, but that's why I came. I am for you, in spite of you, so trust in me."

This is why Luther wrote to Philip Melanchthon these controversial and misunderstood words: "Be a sinner and sin boldly, but believe and rejoice in Christ even more boldly."**

I believe he was saying that a saint is simply a forgiven sinner and sin is inescapable, so cling to Jesus and rejoice in Him who is our victory over sin! He has drowned our sin and satisfies our thirst in the river of His love, which happens as we, in our limited and God-gifted freedom, learn to abide. As A. W. Tozer wrote in his book *The Pursuit of God* (a book I have read every year for a decade): "To have found God and still to pursue Him is the soul's paradox of love."***

*John 13:38–14:1, NIV.

**This quote is from a letter written by Luther to a young, troubled Melanchthon on August 1, 1521. Scott H. Hendrix, *Martin Luther: Visionary Reformer* (New Haven, Conn.: Yale University Press, 2015), 121.

***A. W. Tozer, *The Pursuit of God* (London: Marshall, Morgan & Scott, 1961), 15. Much has been said about A. W. Tozer since his death regarding the essentially ascetic life he lived and how it left his wife feeling neglected. It has raised many questions around how seriously we should take the work of someone whose life was marked by duplicity. If Jesus is sincerely lifted up and Scripture is honored, I am hard-pressed to release books that have deeply blessed me because it has come to light that our spiritual heroes are sinners like everyone else. However, there are things that I have little appetite for, such as listening to voices who utilize Scripture like Acts 6 to argue that their ministry is to pray and study at the expense of life with

. . .

The power and mystery of our healing lie at the center of the Christian message with the One who thirsts for us, the crucified King, Jesus. His thirst is a proclamation over His world, in all of its rebellion, that it is loved. This is why the cross will always be a source of stumbling. It offends everyone without prejudice. The crowd has never stopped jeering, and Jesus has never stopped loving. The Spirit works real freedom in our lives, for the peace we so ardently seek is found in the One who is Himself our peace, Jesus: "But now in Christ Jesus you who once were far off have been brought near by the blood of Christ. For he himself is our peace."*

The problem is we have turned liberty and peace into the removal of suffering, which is why we're never satisfied. I would suggest a more biblical vision of victory in this age of grace: Jesus, who Himself is our peace, has come to set us free from the need to be free from the impossibility of life.

On this side of eternity, it is often in the furnace of our

---

others. I have met too many spiritual leaders that spend way too much time alone, and I must agree with Martin Luther, who said, "The Devil likes to have the Christian alone, for then he can heap him with worries and depression." Heiko A. Oberman, *Luther: Man Between God and the Devil,* trans. Eileen Walliser-Schwarzbart (New York: Doubleday, 1992), 309. An overemphasis on the glory of God at the expense of love for sinful, broken humanity perverts our understanding of God and His Word. With the number of leaders falling today, as I've already stated but will state again, I think the greatest need in the church is for Christians to stop presenting an ideal that they cannot keep.

*Ephesians 2:13–14.

conflict and suffering that His peace and liberation are experienced most fully. Yes, there will be a time when the lion lies down with the lamb, when our tears shall be wiped away, but that, my friends, lies only on the other side of death.

The Big Fella

[2019]

> He is the Love that will not let us go. If anybody can
> sort it all out, he can; if he can't, nobody else ever will.
> Trust him, therefore. And trust him now. There is nothing
> more to do.
>
> —**Robert Farrar Capon,** *Kingdom, Grace, Judgment*

I glanced at the phone in my hand. An unknown
number with a 907 area code appeared. I stood
there in the Orlando airport, waiting to fly home
from a speaking engagement. Anyone who knows
me can attest to my peculiar aversion to answering
my cell phone and even responding to my text messages and emails.* It is unusual for me to answer a
number that I do not recognize.

---

*Apologies and thank you to all those who have worked with me in this
arena. I'm sure at times it has felt like those bad dreams where you cannot
run for some reason. The fact that I just glanced down at my text messages
to see that I have *335* unanswered ones proves my point—I am sure for
some reading this, like my wife, it might cause you a momentary panic
attack.

But 907 is Alaska.

I knew it had to be about Dad. Since he is even worse with his phone than I am, I answered. It wasn't the hospital, as usual, or one of Dad's dysfunctional migratory friends that would call occasionally to tell me Dad was back in the hospital. The man's voice was unfamiliar but kind and clear.

His name was Frank. He was a hospital chaplain who had moved up to Soldotna, Alaska, from the Bay Area with his family to start a church. After struggling to get the church up and going—which, I must say, I can understand after spending time there—he took a job at the hospital. He said that after becoming a chaplain, he realized that this was his calling. He enjoyed ministering to people like my father—those rough and salty off-the-grid types who can't go to church and probably wouldn't if they could. I'll go a step further and say that even if they made it in the door, folks like my dad (who lives on an income of $800 a month) would have very little to give.*

This humble man had died to his dream of being a

*Now I'm curious what my dad could give to a church, so let's do the math. My dad's $800 was spent on: One pizza at $16 per week ($64 per month), a fifth of cheap McCormick vodka at $7.29 per day ($225.99 per month), two packs of Camel Reds at $16 per day ($496 per month), plus tips for the pizza delivery guy who buys the vodka and cigarettes as well at $10 per week ($40 per month). This equals negative $25.99. So I retract my earlier conclusion; folks like my pops would have less than nothing to give.

church planter, and Jesus had resurrected his dream
in a way he could not have foreseen. Now he was a
shepherd to the unwanted, the broken, and the hurting like Alexander.

Frank, on the line thousands of miles from me,
who up to this point had been unknown to me, said
that he had been visiting and sharing with, praying
over, and patiently loving my father for several years.
Then he said these stunning words, "Josh, I hope you
don't mind that I got your number from your dad. He
is here in the hospital but doing good. Sorry if I
alarmed you, but I had to call, and I asked your dad
permission. Al just told me that he prayed to receive
Jesus last week! Can you believe it? Man, he is stub-
born, but I just kept chipping away. I will say, as I
kept asking him questions, I could see he was struggling to trust it."

We talked for a while longer; when I got off the
phone, I sat down in a chair surrounded by a sea of
people. It was as if no one was there. My head was
spinning as the dots began to connect. I had noticed
over the couple of years leading up to this conversation that my dad was able to engage with me on
spiritual matters and even utilize a vocabulary of
faith that baffled me since he had never gone to
church. I now realized that had come from his time
with Frank.

I had felt so much distress over the few years
leading up to this. My dad had been admitted to

the ER and ICU at death's door so many times that
he was on a first-name basis with the entire staff.
Again and again he was nursed back to health at
the hospital. I saw now that had been the perfect
place for God's intervention. In the hospital Dad
was known, touched, cared for, and healed. He
wasn't allowed to drink or smoke, which is why it
was always the place where my conversations with
him were the most consistent and clear. It was his
church, a place where he was not judged but accepted and encouraged. Of course, the doctors,
nurses, and social workers always spoke truth to
him and warned him about his addictions, and
yet every time he came back in the same sad
state, they still received him, no questions asked.
This community is where my dad met God, and
Frank the chaplain had been his pastor there to
guide him.

. . .

I called Dad the next day and told him I had
talked with Frank. Then I asked him about what
happened. He said to me in a weak and tired
voice, "I did ask Jesus to save me and forgive
me . . ."
   "And?"
   "I'm not sure it stuck."
   Man, I loved the honesty in that statement.

"Dad, first of all, if you are worried about your drinking, if you stopped at this point, I am not sure it wouldn't kill you—although I hope you can. Or your smoking, or the fact you feel like you have nothing to contribute. Let me just say Jesus isn't after this or that part of you. He wants you—all of you, the good and the bad. He has been pursuing you and doesn't need your help when it comes to your salvation, just your yes to His! Besides, I am sure His grace is stickier than your doubt!"

He responded to me with a gentle sigh of relieved agreement and said, "I do pray to Him every day, Joshua. But can I ask you a question?"

"Of course, Dad!"

"Is it okay if I call Him the Big Fella?"

I laughed. "As long as you started with Jesus!"

"I did, but that's how I think about Him, the Big Fella! I love you, son."

"I love you too, Dad."

. . .

It is only when we drink from the living water that we will be able to hold on to faith for those that are faithless, love for those that feel unlovable, and hope for those that are hopeless. We can be a revelation of Christ, the thirsty river who brings satisfaction to this restless and hurting world. As Jesus said to the woman at the well, "Whoever drinks of the water that I will give him will never be thirsty again. The water that I will give him will become in him a spring of water welling up to eternal life."*

*John 4:14.

6.

The Cross of the End & Beginning

The Sixth Word from the Cross

When Jesus had received the sour wine,
he said, "It is finished," and he bowed his head
and gave up his spirit.

—John 19:30

Looking to Jesus, the founder and perfecter of our
faith, who for the joy that was set before him endured
the cross, despising the shame, and is seated at the
right hand of the throne of God.

—Hebrews 12:2

What's Done Is Done

My past is everything I failed to be.

—Fernando Pessoa, *The Book of Disquiet*

I glorified you on earth, having accomplished
the work that you gave me to do.

—Jesus, John 17:4

The sixth word brings us toward the close. Its significance cannot be overstated, for it is the very foundation of our faith. There is now nothing that needs to be done that hasn't already been done. As Richard John Neuhaus wrote in his beautiful book on the seven words from the cross, "It is finished, yet it is not over. It is finished means it is settled, decided, certain, complete and incontestable. Consummatum est. Nothing can happen now to undo it."*

He is the *logos,* the Word become event, the author and the finisher of our faith, the first and the last. It is fin-

---

*Richard John Neuhaus, *Death on a Friday Afternoon: Meditations on the Last Words of Jesus from the Cross* (New York: Basic Books, 2001), 191.

ished, but it is not over. This is the word that strikes the final blow to our autonomy—our fiercely independent natures.

It offends our modern sensibilities and declares that our only contribution to salvation is our sin.

I did the sinning. God did the saving.

The Wrath That Healed

[2010–11]

If only I could tell someone.
The humiliation I go through
when I think of my past
can only be described as grace.
We are created by being destroyed.

—Franz Wright, "Letter, January 1998"

August 2010. It was the second year of our church plant, Door of Hope, in the heart of Portland, Oregon, and I found myself in the throes of what one could call a mental breakdown. I prefer "a temporary twilight"; it sounds less ominous.

Something that had lain dormant in me since my early teen years had erupted with a vengeance—anxiety. It manifested out of nowhere, lasted exactly eight months, and its focus (without justification) was on the love of my life—my wife, Darcy—who has always been my greatest gift and idol. I stopped eating, I cried constantly—like a "somebody died" kind of crying. I stopped sleeping. Worst of all, I believed that my wife, much to her bewilderment, didn't love me any longer. This created an endless sense of dread.

To be clear, my wife had *not* stopped loving me. A combination of elements initiated this delusion—a perfect cocktail of unmanaged stress, my glitchy and obsessive constitution, sin, and, I'm sure, spiritual attack. There was not an arena of my marriage that was not profoundly impacted, and my beautiful wife, who was at the center of my obsessive behavior, suffered deeply under its weight. My instability had transformed me, as she called it, into a "human pillow on her face." Without Jesus, I'm not sure she would have stayed. Understandably so.

Paradoxically, this was simultaneously a season of explosive, messy, and beautiful growth for the church. This growth was not primarily caused by people who were leaving one church for another.*

---

*There will always be a plethora of reasons people leave one church to attend another; some are valid and many are not. When a church explodes with transfer growth, it's not a win for anyone. It not only damages the churches that have lost their members, but it will also inevitably lead to a spiritual sickness that can take years to manifest in the church whose growth was built not on conversions but hype. When Door of Hope began, a dear friend and beloved pastor here in Portland said to me (with "tongue firmly planted in cheek") that there is a "three-legged stool" that guarantees growth: A charismatic communicator, great worship, and a well-run children's ministry. He pointed out that all those things can be manufactured without the Spirit— much like a corporation. How have we forgotten that we exist for the good of those who sit outside our walls and not those within the walls of another church? Spirit-filled witness must once again be the focus. Jesus must be lifted up in humility and the power of the Spirit.

For reasons that still lie beyond my understanding, we had become a magnet for the spiritually disenfranchised and dechurched. Like a mysterious thread, young adults who had moved to the city to get away from their religious upbringing were returning to their faith and inviting their nonbelieving friends, who in turn were hearing about and meeting Jesus for the first time, and so on. In a city like Portland, known for its bohemian, progressive, anything-but-church spirit, this was astounding. This was an eccentric era of hyper-hipsterdom, gutter punks, carny folk, dumpster diving—it was never safe to eat pastries during this period at the church—fixed-gear bikes, Pabst beer, mustaches, patchouli, and body odor.

It really was as much of a miracle as it was a carnival. And yet amid this little awakening where God was drawing so many to Himself, I—a carrier of His liberating message—was bound and drowning. The reasons I ended up in this place are too multifaceted to detail. If I were to describe that dark interval, it would be something akin to the words of the mysterious Portuguese poet Fernando Pessoa, "It's as if someone were using my life to beat me with."*

Toward the close of my *dark night of the soul* the Spirit revealed something troubling but necessary:

---

*Fernando Pessoa, *The Book of Disquiet: The Complete Edition* (New York: New Directions, 2017), 11.

The *someone* was in fact the shadow self that Jesus came to set me free from. Our greatest threats tend to come from within. It's a terrifying possibility that we, as Christians, can use our blood-purchased liberty to return to the life He has freed us from. We can cause much harm while thinking we're doing good. I didn't know it at the time, but I had begun to worship my service of the King rather than the King whom I served.

The moment I lost my center all hell broke loose. Like the first thief on the cross, I made demands upon Jesus, and He had nothing to say back to me. I was attempting to use Him to accomplish my dreams, and yet it was cloaked in a spiritual language that was as sincere as it was misguided. Like Nebuchadnezzar, God had struck me with His mercy blow. I felt like I was going to die, and in some ways I did, but it was a good death. It was the necessary corrective that brought me back to the heart of the heart where I found healing. The wrath of God was on display and so was His mercy, as it states in Romans 1 three times: "God gave them over."* God, in His mercy, had given me over to the lie of who He never intended me to be.

In April 2011, my breakthrough came in a place of desperation. I was alone in a cabin, fasting and wrestling with God. I found myself in an open space

*Romans 1:24, 26, 28, NIV.

with the Deschutes River rapidly moving before me. I fell onto my knees sobbing. It was here I saw what I have only experienced a few times in my life: A vision.*

My mind became filled with one image after another of my life since I had come to faith in 1999.

I saw myself reading a Bible—the one my mother had given me on my twenty-first birthday, which had remained unopened until I was twenty-six—alone in

---

*If you're wondering if I am charismatic: I do believe the spiritual gifts are for today, and I have experienced many things that go beyond explanation, such as prophetic words, healing, and exorcisms. I have never thought of the miraculous as a violation of the natural order of things but simply God's gracious and mysterious intervention in a fallen world. Honestly, life itself is as much of a miracle as it is a struggle. Having said that, I do not believe the *focus* of the church should be on signs and wonders any more than it should be focused on fixing societal woes. I'm not looking for healing; I'm looking for the wounded Healer. I'm also not foolishly chasing a peace that will not be found on this side of eternity; I want Jesus who is my peace. It is frustrating to see the Holy Spirit treated like a force to be wielded rather than someone to be surrendered to. He is a missionary Spirit, not a magician. He is also sovereign and is Himself the gift. We are told to desire the gifts, not make demands like spoiled kids. So to answer the question, I must borrow from a friend and fellow pastor, who said to me on a trip to England, "I am charismatic with a seatbelt."

Since I was a boy, I have witnessed those Christian leaders who have capitalized on the technology of the day (from television to the internet), whose claims of healing powers are so commonplace that robbing the grave seems as normative as robbing the widows who watch their ministries. So supernatural—so they claim—are their lives that one is given the impression that even their flatulence carries the healing aroma of Christ. I do my best to stay ambivalent. I wasn't there, but it seems to be the practice of the leaders who live in front of the camera to mysteriously never have it on when these miracles take place. But even if they do, let's say, raise the dead—which God can do if He wants to, even through a con artist—we must remember they still have to die again. If I had gone home to be with Jesus, I'd be more than a little disappointed if I were brought back to a fallen world only to have to die again. I'll take the miracle of the new birth any day of the week over raising the dead.

our tiny apartment on Queen Anne Hill in Seattle. The Word came alive, and I met Jesus.

I saw the small family church in the Wallingford neighborhood by Gas Works Park that met in a middle school. There I was befriended by the pastor. He encouraged me, and he ultimately talked me into leading worship.

I saw myself quitting a band that I had given everything to and going on a mission trip to Smolensk and Ryazan, Russia. There I wrote my first worship song, "The Beauty of Simplicity," and shared Jesus with three young Russians who all came to faith, giving me my first thrill of ministry.

I saw the love of my life, Darcy, in her rocker, holding our son Henry the morning after she gave her life to Christ while nursing in the middle of the night. She didn't say a word; I just looked at her and asked, "What happened?" because she was filled with so much light. The same woman had almost left me over my faith two years earlier.

I saw the music career He gave back to me at the age of twenty-nine when I thought it was all over. I saw the two-hundred-plus shows in one year, which exposed me to every square inch of Christendom in America, some good and some bad, but all of it helpful for what would come. There I was excitedly sharing the gospel and music with thousands around the world. I saw myself in my makeshift bed in the back of our tour van, reading hundreds of books like a kid who had been given the keys to a candy store.

I devoured theology, fiction, history, and the Bible until I thought my head would explode.

I saw the births of Henry and Hattie and the endless pleasure, bottomless love, and sheer pride I felt and still feel in being their father.

I saw Darcy and me starting Door of Hope in the very neighborhood in Portland where we met and fell in love thirteen years earlier to the month. This was the spot we had dreamed of doing ministry, and here we were. We had experienced seven years in ministry—working for three churches in three states and spending one year on the road. Now we were bringing the healing message of Jesus to kids who, just like ourselves in our early adult years, had come to the city idealistic but hungry, lost but hopeful, confused but driven, and carnal but knowing there had to be more. And now at the close of our second year at the church, despite this mental crack, so many had already met Jesus.

Here I was—a guy who grew up with so much trauma, who barely made it out of high school, who spent a decade doing drugs and chasing the rock-and-roll dream to no avail—now at thirty-seven on a river, and the Holy Spirit brought to remembrance the question I had hid in my heart but forgotten. It now burned in me like a holy fire: "Do you not know that God's kindness is meant to lead you to repentance?"*

My heart was overwhelmed with God's goodness,

*Romans 2:4, RSV.

and I cried out two words over and over that I hadn't said in six months, "Thank You! Thank You! Thank You even for this pain! Forgive me! I need You, Lord, more than I need Your healing!"

Jesus, in His intervening mercy, confronted me with the mixture. Like Nebuchadnezzar, I had forgotten who I was, but now God had restored my mind and lifted the cloud. I was free. As painful as it was, and I pray it never happens again, it was what I needed. Humility might be best learned through the school of humiliation. Having come out of that season in the shade of His hand, I can say it is one of the best things that ever happened to me.

Perfect from Now On

Mountain, I do not love you, for you remind me of the
clouds, of the sunset, of the rising sky, and these are things that
almost make me cry because one can never reach them!

—Franz Kafka, *Description of a Struggle*

You therefore must be perfect, as your
heavenly Father is perfect.

—Matthew 5:48

I met with a counselor after seeing my dad to try to understand what I was feeling toward him. I was wrestling through why it was so hard to enter his life while at the same time I could not handle the thought of life without him. I raised what I thought were insightful and self-aware questions, like, "I don't understand why I can't bring myself to call him. I know I can procrastinate on things that sit outside my gifting, but I'm actually really disciplined in the things I love."

With gentle precision, after listening to me ramble for forty minutes in a failed attempt to avoid a hard conversation—I am the master of using vulnerability to disarm people and prevent them from probing any further—he looked at me with a warm smile, and I knew that he knew I was grasping at straws. He simply said, "Josh, you are driven, not disciplined."

Checkmate. He had pushed my self-deception into the open and called it out in six words. I could no longer pretend, at least not in front of this guy, to be the good son, holy pastor, or disciplined saint. This was a beautiful burn, and it helped me begin to come to terms with my own madness and see how desperately I, like everyone, need help.

I can exist in such a state of manic intensity that those casually acquainted with me might be tempted to think that my passion must equal productivity. In actuality, it is the obsessive fear of the unfinished event, the drive to know all, and the desire to enjoy and experience all that can keep me slogging through life. That is a whimsical way of describing what most of us struggle with most of the time: Trust. Even as I write these words, I am convicted by the question, "Is it really the fear of missing out that drives this manic activity?" I feel the Spirit of truth pricking my conscience in this moment and gently, but firmly, asking, "Is it the fear of the unfinished event or is it the unaddressed relational brokenness and fear of pain that keeps you in this state?"

If that isn't bad enough, I can shift without warning, moving from manic engagement to emotional detachment. I become what the French poet Charles Baudelaire called the *flâneur,* "the passionate observer . . . [of] the world, and yet . . . unseen of the world,"* one who has a keen eye for poetic observation but often little appetite for intimacy. I can be emotionally impenetrable. My wife calls this state "the shell." I have come to recognize how often I can overwhelm a space or be lost in space. It's probably fair to say I have a tendency toward the extreme. I can move from obsessive recklessness, turning myself into a "suffocating pillow," to emotional detachment, reducing myself to a "phantom." I am wearied just writing these words, which press down with the weight of some kind of cosmic indictment.

Oh, who will save me from this body of death?**

When we read a phrase like "Be holy," does it not feel suspiciously like a cloaked instruction to try harder? Please know, I am not challenging the authority of Scripture—just its interpretation. I am also not saying do nothing, but often the something we do to achieve the holiness we do not understand amounts to nothing. I have watched too many people I love over the last twenty years of ministry abandon their faith, and I have lost sleep and wept over the very real possibility that I may have, for some, contributed to that demise. This has led to the solemn conviction that the lies we believe and the truths we avoid do not hurt us without hurting others.

We are not bigger failures than God already knows we are. (I'm not trying to be offensive.) It is true, and that is

*Charles Baudelaire, *The Painter of Modern Life* (London: Penguin, 2010), 12.

**See Romans 7:24.

why He came. Only through the reception of grace and the release of control can we be freed from the tyranny of the self-centered shadow self. In Jesus, we are reminded that God is not just a God of words, He is a God of action. Jesus is the *logos*—the Word in action. His cross is the greatest revelation of this fact.

The cross is our coup de grâce;* it is our continual corrective. For every fatal blow it wields upon the various arenas of human futility, resurrection life is the outcome. The cross is our center. Jesus did not come to help fulfill our dreams but to bring life to our dead bodies and set us free from the need to be free of life's struggles. The good news hinges upon how good God is toward us despite how good we are not.

*Blow of mercy, or mercy blow.

The Ladder & the Cross

Chutes and Ladders was perhaps the most sadistic board game
ever invented. Adults loathed the game; children loved it.
The universe thus dictated that an adult invariably got
snookered into playing the game with a child.

—David Foster Wallace, *The Broom of the System*

Falling while trying to climb is always frustrating and
sometimes fatal. What about trying to climb from a place
of fallenness? Well, the goal is no longer simply frustrating, it's elusive. Actually, it's impossible. This is the unflinching proclamation of Scripture, yet we don't really
believe it. Our unbelief does not change the cold, hard
fact of sin's impact upon human potential: "For all have
sinned and fall short of the glory of God."*

Sin is written into the fabric of history, collectively and
personally, and it is anchored in the archetypal story of
Babel. It is evidenced by the wasteland of failed attempts
to build to the heavens only to find the foundation faulty
and the destination unobtainable. It's like an endless and

*Romans 3:23.

exhausting game of Chutes and Ladders. We climb and slide, only to start all over again.

Although the details of our lives vary, on this side of eternity, this reality binds us together without prejudice. We want so desperately to believe we can climb our way out of this mess, but every attempt leads, inevitably, to frustration, confusion, exhaustion, and despair.

The gravitational pull on the human heart is not toward total surrender but toward the illusion of untapped potential. Climbing ladders seems to be the default setting of human existence. It's the shared belief that our freedom can only be found in the heroic journey. The world calls it self-improvement; the church often confuses it with spiritual formation. It's the hunger to arrive, to find the silver bullet to wholeness.* Some secret knowledge that will guide us step-by-step out of whatever difficulty we have found ourselves in, leading us into the proverbial promised land of fulfillment. There really does seem to be

---

*It isn't surprising that this hunger has created an eleven-billion-dollar self-help industry and that Christian authors are adding to this genre daily. *Your Best Life Now* is an easy target, but what about the soon-to-be-out-of-vogue millennial Christian obsession with Enneagram titles? If you've never heard of the Enneagram, save yourself the journey, that ultimately, from my very biased view, leads not toward the cross, surrender, and Jesus but to the ladder of self-discovery and independence. My hunch is that the legalism of eighties and nineties evangelicalism that demonized things like Halloween and Harry Potter has created a stunted "rebellious child" phenomenon among a generation that grew up in the church. (By the way, to my knowledge, reading Rowling has never created a real wizard—though, well, maybe in Portland.) Now this generation is demanding the right to dabble in the occult and pop psychology. Equipped with nine magic numbers, an upside-down pentagram, and a mysterious, opaque, very suspect origin story that is bathed in pseudo-Catholic mysticism and Gnosticism, this generation has been granted the secret power to understand themselves and read others with absolute precision. When people ask for my number, my answer aligns with Scripture: A zero.

a ladder for everything. No matter what fantastical distance one must go, how exhausting the climb or implausible the promise, climbing and falling will always be preferred to repenting and dying, even if dying is the key to actually living.

The cross will always be a source of stumbling as we brave this life and move toward eternity because it doesn't yield to demands for bargaining, and it is the great equalizer of existence. It is the supreme revelation of holy love colliding with human impotence. The cross is the eternal reminder that we have nothing to bring to the table but our surrender. This undermines our control and exposes our mixture.

Sadly, even as I write this, I cringe at how often I am still bitten by this hard word. I know real freedom is found by coming into the light, but it is painful because I don't like my idols and weaknesses exposed more than anyone else does. Sometimes, it's just too costly, the path too narrow, and my flesh too lazy, so I wander, looking for some semblance of certainty in everything but the One who is truly certain, Jesus. He has finished the work and invited me into the impossible possibility of His wholeness. And yet so often, in the freedom that flows from His perfection, I return to the climb, repeating what the apostle Paul so clearly condemned when he asked the church of Galatia, "Having begun by the Spirit, are you now being perfected by the flesh?"*

*Galatians 3:3.

He was asking, "Why are you negating the Spirit's application of Jesus's perfection to your lives by attempting to add to what is already perfect?" His work can't be improved upon, but it can be missed; it cannot be diminished, but it can be rejected. A life of freedom will never be found climbing ladders. The gospel is down-to-earth with the cross of Christ at its center.

The cross is not something to climb. It is something to die on. Again and again.

There is only one mention of a ladder in the Bible, and that is in the mysterious vision of Jacob whose very name means *deceiver*. Yet God choose him to be the one by whom He would move His redemptive history forward. This is the same Jacob who deceived his dying and blind father, Isaac, into believing he was Esau and stole his brother's blessing. He deceived his brother, Esau, into giving up his birthright and then fled for his life. He is the same shifty character who deceived his uncle Laban and ultimately wrestled with God Himself before receiving a new name: Israel. In Genesis 28, God makes a covenant—*an immovable promise*—with Jacob in a dream, and God spoke to him from the top of a ladder that reached from earth to the heavens.

> And he dreamed, and behold, there was a ladder
> set up on the earth, and the top of it reached to
> heaven. And behold, the angels of God were as-
> cending and descending on it! And behold, the
> LORD stood above it. . . . Then Jacob awoke from

his sleep and said, "Surely the LORD is in this
place, and I did not know it."*

The mystery of the dream is not in the covenantal
promise God makes with Jacob but in the ladder, which
is a revelation of the insurmountable distance between
God and humanity due to the fall. The ladder also points
us to the fulfillment of the promise. Two thousand years
later, when Jesus appeared on the scene, He brought an
answer to the "how" and the mystery of the ladder. At the
close of John 1, when Jesus was speaking to Nathanael,
He said, "Truly, truly, I say to you, you will see heaven
opened, and the angels of God ascending and descend-
ing on the Son of Man."**

He is the ladder, and it is in Him, by Him, and for Him
that we are saved—in spite of the mixture that moves us,
often with imperceptible speed, from folly to wisdom, escape to engagement, apathy to care, and even idolatry to
worship. Yes, in Him real joy and peace are found. In the
acceptance of His love and our impotence, His radical
grace collides with our crippling brokenness. Our struggle is the reason He came, and it is in His cross that we
find the paradox of death in life and life in death.

*Genesis 28:12–13, 16.

**John 1:51.

The Ache in My Chest

[2021]

The truth will set you free. But not until it is finished with you.

—David Foster Wallace, *Infinite Jest*

October 2021. It was a crisp and clear fall day. Evening was approaching and the sky out our kitchen window displayed varying shades of orange, lavender, and pink, which stood out against the technicolor green of the verdant landscape. My phone sat on the counter before me as I visited with Darcy. It was silenced but vibrating. His name appeared on the screen: Al "Dad."

It was the third call in two days. Darcy looked down at the phone and then at me. I knew what was coming and glanced over my shoulder to the quickly darkening sky to hide my discomfort.

"Honey, are you going to answer this time?"

I couldn't do it. "I promise I'll call him before I go to bed."

That decision, as with so many over the years, was avoidance under the guise of good intentions. As I lay in bed, I listened, with a dull ache in my chest, to that sad and familiar voice. It was marked by his usual economy of language—a twelve-word request, accompanied by his unusual addition of *s*'s to words when he drinks, which created the illusion of an accent: "Yeah, Joshua, it's your dad. Gives me a call when yous can. Okays. Mm, bye . . ." Then I heard a shuffling sound, followed by a click.

I saved it. He communicates so much through so little. His few words flowed from a lonely space. He was commandeered by a body whose incompleteness acted like a death grip on his heart and a hammer blow on his mind.

I want to be very careful to not leave the impression that I have figured out the key to conquering one's childhood traumas—we cannot forget the principle of mixture. I may have a strong mental grasp of what the gospel is and believe in it deeply, but can I honestly say I know the truth if it is not loved and lived? What is heartbreaking about my relationship with my dad is that though we have made much progress over the last ten years, I still find myself selfishly avoiding him, and he me. I know my dad is dying, sitting in his mildew-infested, smoke-stained cabin, unbathed, barely sleeping, drinking and smoking, finding relationships with shows that are as absent from the collective mind today as he is.* He does have a roommate now, who I am sure is nearly as dysfunctional as my father. Still, I am relieved he is not alone—but I am not there. I haven't seen him since before the pandemic, and I haven't talked to him in three months. When he gets depressed, he stops answering his phone and stops calling. It's a vicious cycle. Darcy finds my in-action unbearable and protests often, having lost so many that are dear to her. She said, "Honey, I don't want you to have regrets! You are all he has, and he needs you. Please call your dad before you get the call he is gone!"

Gone? That's the problem. He was never there, and I needed him. Then the cold logic of my mem-ory wounds crumble because he is up there in that coming Alaskan darkness that stunts the soul like the permafrost stunts the trees. But still, I can't do it, so I tell myself, *I'll call him tomorrow.* I sometimes won-der if procrastination, like with writing this book, is ever laziness for me, or is it the suffering of past trauma that produces the agony of the act? All I know is it's too much—the drunken repetition, the fragmented nostalgia. But that's not the problem ei-ther. This cold in my soul flows from the fact that I

---

*His primary diet is *Bonanza, Little House on the Prairie, The Waltons, Mag-num, P.I.,* and occasionally Fox News. When I asked him why, he answered, "Because they are good people." With the exception of the news, I believe he is either drawn to a sense of family he once knew or, more likely, the family he wished he had.

can't fix him. Actually, I think it's deeper still: I'm as afraid of his looming death as he is. I can hardly handle the death in his voice, the forced breathing, the rattle in his cough, the extinguished vitality. But most of all it's the thought of losing him—my stranger father.

What is once and for all with Jesus must be played out in real time for us, and it can seem as impossible as life itself. But that's the point, isn't it? Life is terminally impossible, and I know the strength I need will not be achieved by my own "willpower." The fact is I have no power to will, and it doesn't matter because I can't stop what, in our modernity, we have learned to deny so fully—death. As Philip Larkin wrote with such unsettling honesty in his great poem "Aubade,"

> Courage is no good:
> It means not scaring others. Being brave
> Lets no one off the grave.
> Death is no different whined at than withstood.*

What I need, what we all need, is the reminder that even though Jesus has not extinguished the pain of this human comedy, He has permanently dismantled death's finality and promises to carry us through it. I can surrender to the gentle grace of Jesus, and in

*Philip Larkin, "Aubade," in *Collected Poems* (New York: Farrar, Straus and Giroux, 2004).

the power of the Spirit, I can walk through the shadow of death with Dad. God's will must be my rule, and if His desire is that all people be saved, I can leave that mystery with Him. I can be a witness, but I can no more save Alexander—or anyone for that matter—than I can prevent his death, but I can call him, love him, and remind him in his bullhead-edness that he is divinely loved. I can comfort him in his suffering, be patient with him in his brokenness, and walk with him through the valley of the shadow of death as we stumble toward eternity together.

The victory cry of Jesus on the cross changed everything forever. Death will not have the last word. It may be finished, but for us here and now, it is not over yet.

7.

The Cross of Surrender & Rest

The Seventh Word from the Cross

It was now about the sixth hour, and there was darkness over the whole land until the ninth hour, while the sun's light failed. And the curtain of the temple was torn in two. Then Jesus, calling out with a loud voice, said, "Father, into your hands I commit my spirit!" And having said this he breathed his last. Now when the centurion saw what had taken place, he praised God, saying, "Certainly this man was innocent!"

—Luke 23:44–47

Last Words & the Paragon

On the seventh day God finished his work that he had done, and
he rested on the seventh day from all his work that he had done.
So God blessed the seventh day and made it holy, because on it
God rested from all his work that he had done in creation.

—Genesis 2:2–3

Last words are mysterious and will often illuminate the
heart of the individual who speaks them. Sometimes they
can be . . .

incomplete like Mark Twain. After speaking to his
daughter Clara, he asked for a pencil and wrote,
"Give me my glasses."*

scared like singer Amy Winehouse, whose final
words were "I don't want to die."**

*"Mark Twain's Last Words," *Manchester Guardian,* April 22, 1910.

**Marilyn Mendoza, "A Collection of Last Words," *Psychology Today,* April 4, 2017.

humorous like Groucho Marx, who joked, "Die,
my dear? Why that is the last thing I'd do."*

angry like Sigmund Freud, who said, "Now it is
nothing but torture and makes no sense anymore."**

heartbreaking like Chris Farley, who cried out to
the call girl who he had spent the weekend with,
"Don't leave me."***

courageous and beautiful like Thomas Cranmer,
archbishop of Canterbury, who was marched out
to burn at the stake on March 21, 1556. It is recorded he plunged his right hand into the heart of
the flames, calling it an "unworthy . . . hand." His
last words were, "Lord Jesus, receive my spirit. . . .
I see the heavens open and Jesus standing at the
right hand of God."*****

Yet in the words of Jesus, we find something more—
something profound—for here at the close of His torment
there is confidence, full control, and peace. This is the
death of death and the birth of rest. Yes, there is a rest that
only God can provide, and it flows from the holiness of
this moment. Here in the valley of trouble Jesus secured
our rest. As Martin Luther wrote in his Heidelberg Dispu-

---

*Mendoza, "A Collection of Last Words."

**Mendoza, "A Collection of Last Words."

***Tom Farley, Jr., and Tanner Colby, *The Chris Farley Show: A Biography in Three
Acts* (New York: Viking, 2008), 312.

****John Foxe, *Foxe's Book of Martyrs* (Start Publishing, 2012), 189.

tation, "The law says, 'do this,' and it is never done. Grace says, 'believe in this,' and everything is already done."*

Like the close of the creation account, the work has been finished. It cannot be improved upon. Salvation has come, and rest is forever secured. He is the One stronger than the strong man. He has pillaged the kingdom of darkness and defeated sin. Jesus left His glory and went into the depths of the outer darkness to set the captives free. Now He, like the prodigal son, has returned to His Father and placed Himself in His hand as an emblem of total victory over death itself and the paragon of total surrender.

*Gerhard O. Forde, *On Being a Theologian of the Cross: Reflections on Luther's Heidelberg Disputation, 1518* (Grand Rapids, Mich.: Eerdmans, 1997), 107.

Home

[February 8, 2022]

> But there are no happy endings, because if things are happy they have not ended.
>
> **—Donald Hall,** *Essays After Eighty*

Time may carry an internal logic that is consistent within itself, but for we who live within its boundaries, the only thing that feels consistent is its inconsistency. How we talk about the succession of life communicates our experience of time rather than what time actually is. We connect descriptors to it or personify it: Too much *time,* not enough *time,* your *time* is up, the *time* got away from me, *time* has aged him, *time* seemed to stop, if only we could turn back *time,* and so on. All I can say about time on this side of eternity is that for each of us, it is simply the space between our appointed beginning and end.

As the preacher of Ecclesiastes declared, "For everything there is a season, and a time for every mat-

ter under heaven: a time to be born, and a time to
die."*

. . .

Dad had escaped death so many times I thought
maybe it had forgotten him. It hadn't. I know because I was there, staring into his eyes when the *appointed time* came, and he was gone. His *time* was
up, while mine left him behind, and I still can't get
my head around it.

   He died at 3 P.M. If I had been in Portland—
where the time zone is an hour earlier than
Anchorage—at the same *time,* I could've had one
more hour with him alive. But I wouldn't have been
with him when his *time* came, and that's not how it
works anyway. How can anyone be prepared for the
close of someone's story? Whether we are the ones
dying or watching others die, there is a curtain up
that will not be penetrated except by the one who
passes through it. In *Walking to Martha's Vineyard,*
poet Franz Wright, who fought with cancer and lost
(but found his faith in the process from what little I
can tell), wrote this passage that has haunted me,
reflecting on how no one can teach us how to die
because

*Ecclesiastes 3:1–2.

The world
is filled with people
who have never died*

. . .

What happens when the heart stops may be an impenetrable mystery, but how we face death is something we can and should talk about. For the Christian, our courage and hope is derived from the core conviction that Jesus conquered death and is, now and forever, the crucified and risen King.

This is the source of our hope, and it is fundamental to our belief that the *end of time* as we know it will only be the beginning. The best is yet to come. But that doesn't change the fact that death, though defeated, is still an enemy that wounds us deeply. Everyone must pass through it.

. . .

At 6 P.M. on February 7, I received the call from the hospital. Dad was once again in the ER. I had power of attorney and permissions were needed from me to move forward with any procedures for my father. I had talked to this doctor many times before, but he

---

*Franz Wright, *Walking to Martha's Vineyard: Poems* (New York: Knopf, 2005), 4.

was different this time—hesitant. Finally, he said slowly, "Josh, your dad's internal organs are shutting down. He is very sick, and I think it would be cruel to intubate him. I feel it's time that we put him on comfort care."

No matter how true that statement was, to give a doctor that I did not know permission to let my father die was an unbearable responsibility. It did not feel like it should be mine to give that permission. I wanted to say, "How can I give you that? I'm not God."

But I knew if Alexander could not decide for himself, it had to be me. "All right, Doctor. How long do I have?"

"He could go within a few hours, but knowing the resilience of your father, my guess is that he will survive at least through the night. But I can't tell you with any certainty."

I hung up shell-shocked and overwhelmed. Darcy embraced me. Her ability to enter the pain of others is unmatched by anyone I've ever met. Time seemed to slow in her arms, and then suddenly it rushed forward . . .

By 6:20 P.M., I had booked the flight to Anchorage from Seattle. It would leave at 10 P.M.

I was on the road by 6:30 P.M., making the three-hour drive in a record two and a half hours.

I caught the flight with a half hour to spare. Time slowed again until the plane landed at 3:30 A.M.

I caught the second flight from Anchorage to Kenai at 6 A.M.

At 6:30 A.M. I walked by the familiar stuffed Kodiak bear, frozen inside the timeless diorama on the way to the rental car.

By 6:40 A.M. I was out in the permanent twilight of the Alaskan morning—everything white and black. There was a blizzard outside. I drove as quickly as possible through the winter landscape toward the hospital where Dad, Alexander, lay dying.

. . .

At 7 A.M. I walked into his room, and there he was—my stranger father. He had been bathed. His hair was combed back, long, and his beard was the unruliest I had ever seen it—it was the only gray hair on his sixty-nine-year-old body. The only evidence that he was in horrible shape were the sores on his legs that poked out from underneath the bedsheets, which I quickly covered. To be honest, it was the best he had looked in a decade. He seemed like a man prepared for a funeral. There was no bad smell, just soft light and the sound of the various medical devices monitoring his demise.

. . .

Here he was, closing his earthly pilgrimage among his people: Frank the chaplain, the doctors, and the multitude of lovely nurses—young and old—that cared for him. They patiently endured the stench of him not bathing for a month at a time and the internal deterioration of his organs that seemed to seep through his skin. They endured his loss of coherence due to the lack of oxygen and his isolation and withdrawals that would cause him to often lash out, panic, and maybe even cry. The women there even tolerated his relentless offers—regardless of how young or old—to take them out on dates when he could walk again, which, of course, he never did. After my dad passed, one of the young nurses came in and kissed his forehead. She said, "I'm gonna miss you, old-timer. I guess I don't get that date you promised."

I was embarrassed and moved. All of them seemed to truly value him. All I can say is that the church could learn a lot about how to care for people by observing that group. This was his church, and I will be forever grateful to them for the care they provided my father.

. . .

I walked over to the side of the bed. I had written and recorded a song called "Home" the week before, so I pulled it up on my phone and set it next to his head as he slept. As the song began to play, I ran my hand across his warm forehead and took his hand—worn, with those cigarette-stained fingers—

into my own illustrated hand. I bowed my head and prayed, "Thank You, Lord, for letting me be here. I needed to be here."

I was too physically tired to cry, but he was not. As my voice carried from the song, it brought him out of his morphine-induced slumber. He squeezed my hand tight. Tears rolled down his face. I moved my face closer to his and said, "It's okay, Dad. I'm here. I love you. It's okay."

He squeezed my hand to let me know he understood as the tears increased. He tried to open his mouth, but he couldn't talk. He tried to see me, but he couldn't open his eyes. But I was there, his son, and his grip tightened as if he were hanging between this side and the other of his *appointed time* like a man too scared to depart. The nurse came in. I asked Dad if he was hurting, and he squeezed my hand to let me know that he was. He received relief and moved back into his dying sleep, while I watched his breathing become more and more shallow—as if his body was being compressed by death itself. *Time* continued to remind me of what was coming.

. . .

At 3 P.M. the nurse told me Dad was close and left me alone. What an appropriate word; he was close to the close of his *time*. The lengthening spaces between each breath gave the impression that he was dying with every refusal of the body to release the last breath that it took in. I put on my song again and his eyelids lifted as soon as my voice, which felt like it belonged to someone else, sang the words,

> Some days I just fall apart
> So many worries haunt this heart
> Some days I don't know where to start
> Some days I can lose you in the dark . . .

I stood over him with my face no more than a foot from his and stared straight into his fading, fearful eyes. He began to weep again. His distress from his inability to breathe was unbearable to watch, and I wanted to look away; I couldn't help him, and yet I was. I touched his cheek and told him it was okay, that it was time. It may seem like a strange thing to say to someone who is about to close out their journey through time as we know it, but life is a gift, and it does not surrender itself easily.

The look changed on his face, and he began to become calm as I sang the words of the bridge,

> Remind me that it's all right to cry
> Remind me if I hurt, I'm alive
> Remind me that you're by my side
> Remind me that the light makes darkness
> hide . . .

The words of the final chorus released into the ether,

Home, will you guide me home
Oh, tell me I'm not alone

And in ten holy seconds before the closing lines,
he slowly surrendered his last breath and was gone.
His tears had ceased and mine continued as I listened in a disassociated state to my own voice,
which seemed as far away as my father:

Some days I can tear through your world
Rip apart our love without a word
Some days I'm surprised when I wake up
To open up my eyes to your touch.

. . .

The details of what followed are not necessary, but
that experience in that room with my father was holy
and brought to me the clarity needed to finish this
book, a book I had toiled over for two years but
could not complete.

For me, the seventh word from the cross could not
be analyzed. It had to be experienced. What I discovered in that moment with my dad is that the presence of the living Christ, who can feel as elusive to
me as anyone else, made Himself known in a way I
have rarely experienced before. Why? Because, as I
have been saying through this whole little book, His
peace (which is Himself) is rarely found in the ab-

sence of life's difficulties; it's found in the middle of it.

This is why we stumble toward eternity; because the upside-down kingdom of Jesus, who is our peace, is most fully experienced in what we try so desperately to avoid: *Suffering.*

Remember: No cross, no Christ.

When I was willing to enter my dad's suffering, look into his dying eyes and not look away, I found my peace. Jesus was with me. And it is my deepest conviction that what my dad experienced as he looked into my eyes, man of mixture that I am, was Jesus Himself.

This is a great mystery. But I believe that Christ's words from the cross became Alexander's experience. Words that transformed his Valley of Achor—trouble—into a door of hope.*

Forgiveness.

Acceptance.

Comfort.

Belonging.

Intimacy.

Satisfaction.

Victory.

Final rest.

Yes, I was there when his appointed time came, when his last tears rolled and mine began, as he was

*Hosea 2:15.

carried by that defeated foe, death itself, to the home where I will one day find him whole.

Without the cross, that home would be as impossible to reach as Jacob's ladder would be to climb. But the good news has always been down-to-earth, God in Jesus, come down to us. The pilgrimage of Jesus into the depths of our lost state was an invasion of the love of God itself that has come to set the captives—you and me—free. His cross is His victory over sin, death, and the dominions of darkness. His cross is our door of hope and the continual reminder that the best is yet to come.

> Let not your hearts be troubled. Believe in God; believe also in me. In my Father's house are many rooms. If it were not so, would I have told you that I go to prepare a place for you? And if I go and prepare a place for you, I will come again and will take you to myself, that where I am you may be also.*

*John 14:1–3.

In Loving Memory of Alexander Carl White
June 27, 1952–February 8, 2022

© Photography by James Fitzgerald III

JOSH WHITE is a speaker, recording artist, writer, and the founding pastor of Door of Hope, a thriving church community in the heart of Portland.

He has recorded multiple worship albums, including as the frontman of Telecast, and produced and written records for other artists, including Liz Vice's first album, *There's a Light*.

In May 1996, Josh met his wife, Darcy, at the now defunct Satyricon nightclub in Portland. They have two beautiful children, and since 2007, they have been living in the city where they fell in love.